THE AEGEAN MISSION

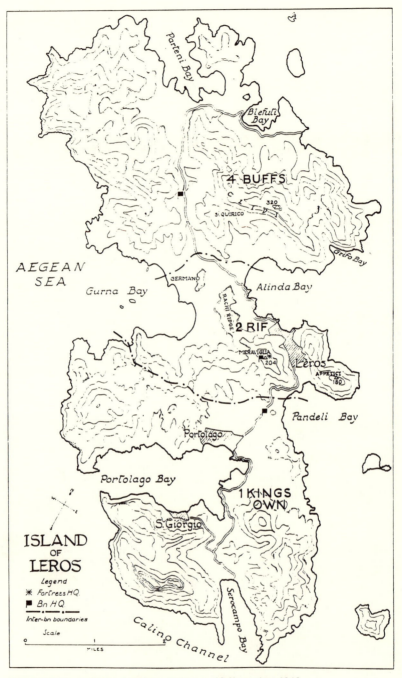

British infantry battalion positions on Leros, 12 November 1943.

THE AEGEAN MISSION

Allied Operations in the Dodecanese, 1943

JEFFREY HOLLAND

Foreword by
Major-General David Lloyd Owen CB, DSO, OBE, MC

Contributions in Military Studies, Number 77

Greenwood Press
New York • Westport, Connecticut • London

Library of Congress Cataloging-in-Publication Data

Holland, Jeffrey.
  The Aegean mission : Allied operations in the Dodecanese, 1943 /
Jeffrey Holland ; foreword by David Lloyd Owen.
    p.   cm. — (Contributions in military studies, ISSN 0883-6884
; no. 77)
  Bibliography: p.
  Includes index.
  ISBN 0-313-26283-7 (lib. bdg. : alk. paper)
  1. World War, 1939-1945—Campaigns—Dodecanese. 2. Dodecanese—
History. I. Title. II. Series.
D766.32.D63H65   1988
940.54'21—dc19   88-5659

British Library Cataloguing in Publication Data is available.

Library of Congress Catalog Card Number: 88-5659
ISBN: 0-313-26283-7
ISSN: 0883-6884

First published in 1988

Greenwood Press, Inc.
88 Post Road West, Westport, Connecticut 06881

Printed in the United States of America

(∞)™

The paper used in this book complies with the
Permanent Paper Standard issued by the National
Information Standards Organization (Z39.48-1984).

10 9 8 7 6 5 4 3 2 1

Copyright Acknowledgments

The author and publisher gratefully acknowledge permission to use portions of the following copyrighted and personal material:

Winston S. Churchill, *The Hinge of Fate: The Second World War*, 6 vols. (Boston: Houghton, Mifflin, 1950), by permission of Houghton, Mifflin and Cassell, London.

Winston S. Churchill, *Closing the Ring: The Second World War* (Boston: Houghton, Mifflin, 1951), by permission of Houghton, Mifflin and Cassell, London.

Forrest C. Pogue, *George C. Marshall: Organizer of Victory, 1943-45* (New York: The Viking Press, 1973), by permission of Viking-Penguin, Inc.

John Coleville, *The Fringes of Power* (London: Hodder & Stoughton, 1985), courtesy of Sir John Coleville.

Max Hastings, *Bomber Command* (London: Michael Joseph, 1979), courtesy of Max Hastings.

David Irving, *Hitler's War* (New York: The Viking Press, 1985), courtesy of David Irving.

Letter from Brigadier Guy L. Prendergast to author, 6 October 1985, courtesy of Mrs. Angela Prendergast and Peter L. Prendergast.

Letter from Brigadier R. A. Tilney to Mrs. Diana French, 1 January 1946, courtesy of Mrs. Diana French.

Letter from Jack Dimetriadis to author, 3 September 1985, courtesy of George Dimitriadis.

Letter from Robert Butler to author, 4 June 1985, courtesy of Robert Butler.

The author and publisher are also grateful for the use of the following photographs:

Photograph of the Mediterranean Commanders, Plate 1, by permission of The Trustees of the Imperial War Museum, London.

Photograph of Stalag VIIA, No. 1345906, by permission of The Trustees of the Imperial War Museum, London.

Photograph of an article in the *Daily Telegraph and Morning Post,* courtesy of Max Hastings, editor, *Daily Telegraph.*

Photograph of the *P-38 Lightnings,* Smithsonian Institution Photo No. 29227/40806 A. C., by permission of the Smithsonian Institution.

Photograph of *HMS Pathfinder,* courtesy of Captain C. W. Malins, RN.

Contents

Part IV   Appendices

Illustrations

Foreword

The conflict between political and strategic considerations that influenced Allied operations in the Dodecanese in 1943 shapes the main narrative of this book. In THE AEGEAN MISSION the author has provided an enthralling and fascinating account of political disingenuousness which, had it been allowed to continue, arguably could have worked to the detriment of Allied operations in the Mediterranean and Europe.

In the summer of 1943, the Allies formulated a plan to menace the coastline of southern Europe in order to deflect German formations from Russia and western France. The Allied invasion of Sicily and Italy and the threat of invasion in southern France were the principal means to achieve these ends. Meanwhile, a plan of deception with the code name ZEPPELIN was designed to mislead the enemy into thinking that the Allies' real intention was to attack through the Balkans instead of in Sicily, as a springboard for the offensive on the Italian Peninsula.

The evidence shows, however, that from 1940 onward, Winston Churchill was, indeed, obsessed with the idea of bringing Turkey into the War. This suggests more than a broad stratagem of deception intended to disguise Allied intentions in northwestern Europe and in the central Mediterranean. Throughout, the Prime Minister used every conceivable argument to induce Turkey to become a co-belligerent.

The commitment and subsequent loss of one-third of the entire British Mediterranean Fleet in the Aegean, together with a complete Infantry Brigade in the Dodecanese, was the price that had to be paid in an abortive attempt to secure what was at best a tangential objective: a commitment by Turkey to enter the War on the Allied side.

With the clear insight of a historian's eye and with direct reference to primary sources of information, Jeffrey Holland has searched through a web of intrigue, incompetence, fantasy and cover-up to find the truth. It is a compelling

story, for, although he records all the relevant facts that can
be established today, there are still many questions unanswered
and on which judgments ultimately will be made.

Why, for example, was Winston Churchill mesmerized by a desire
to open another supply route to Russia through the Dardanelles
when the Combined Chiefs of Staff at the Quebec Conference had
already agreed that the first essential was to knock Italy out
of the War and that operations in the Balkans would be limited
to small scale commando raids and assistance to partisans while
maintaining the strategic bombing offensive?

Why did General Sir Henry Maitland Wilson and the
Commanders-in-Chief of the Middle East succumb to the relentless
political pressure of Winston Churchill and Anthony Eden to
prosecute operations in the Aegean when General Eisenhower and
the Allied commanders in Algiers had already agreed that they
must be abandoned in favor of our objectives in Italy? Why
after the fall of Kos on 4 October did we hold onto Leros and
Samos until they were wrenched from us on 16 November?

All responsible commanders accepted that it was militarily
impossible to defend and maintain these islands without
possession of Rhodes. Leros had no airfield and was never
essential to us anyway. Why, even after the fall of Leros, did
the Prime Minister pursue his Turkish chimera, promising fifty
squadrons of fighter planes, five light AA regiments, five heavy
AA regiments, five anti-tank regiments, and two armored divisions
to the Turks--resources that were never available to him?

This book is a brilliantly researched study of these and many
other enigmatic questions that may never be answered about a
tragic and almost unknown aspect of the Second World War. The
Aegean Mission makes a valuable contribution toward the
literature of World War II, focusing as it does on the political
influences which precipitated such humiliating losses to British
forces in the Middle East, in a campaign that never could have
had a positive effect on the avowed Allied strategy in the
Mediterranean.

The book vividly portrays the tension between American and
British perspectives on the significance of the Mediterranean in
the coalition's strategy for the war against Germany. The story
will appeal to the general reader interested in the history of
World War II and will be of particular use to students of
military science who are concerned with the exercise of power and
the resolution of political conflict.

David Lloyd Owen
Swainsthorpe, Norwich

Acknowledgments

This book could not have been written without the help and guidance of many people. First and foremost, I wish to thank Andrea Duncan, MA, for her splendid assistance. She researched and compiled a voluminous amount of material from the British Public Record Office. Equally, I am grateful to Colonel Paul L. Miles, Department of History, United States Military Academy, West Point, for his definitive critique of the manuscript.

I am indebted to Captain WF Chatterton Dickson, RN, Christopher Bellamy, Jonathan Reed, and Eugene Kolesnik, for their editorial comments. In particular, I am most grateful to Mildred Vasan, Military Studies Editor, Greenwood Press, Inc., for her counsel and confidence in the story and the dedication she has brought to the project.

Thanks are due to Dale Hurst for the original typescript; to Meena Dwivedy and my wife, Eileen, for typing and formatting the camera ready copy; and to my son, Jeremy, who provided useful comments throughout successive iterations of the work. A special word of thanks is due to Elizabeth Hovinen, copy editor for her impeccable editing of the typescript and to Alicia Merritt in dealing with the production process.

References to unpublished sources indicate the nature of the authority for statements of fact or opinions and a specific source when there seemed special reasons for citing the primary source of data. In addition to documents in the public domain, the research has been enriched by reference to published works listed in the bibliography. Judgment on the actions of political figures and military commanders may not reflect the truth behind the perceived reality of their reasoning or conduct under the stress of war. It is all too easy for an author to be wrong. The responsibility for any errors of fact, serious omissions, or expressions of opinion is mine.

Abbreviations

ACM	Air Chief Marshal.
AFHQ	Allied Force Headquarters.
AOC	Air Officer Commanding.
CCS	Combined Chiefs of Staff (Anglo-US).
CIC	Commander(s) in Chief (British).
CIGS	Chief of the Imperial General Staff.
COS	Chiefs of Staff (British).
CRA	Chief, Royal Artillery.
DLI	Durham Light Infantry.
DZ	Dropping Zone.
FUP	Forming Up Position.
GAF	German Air Force.
JIC	Joint Intelligence Committee (of the COS).
JPS	Joint Planning Staff (of the COS).
JSM	Joint Staff Mission.
LMG	Light Machine Gun.
LRDG	Long Range Desert Group.
LSI	Landing Ship Infantry.
LST	Landing Ship Tank.
MAC	Mediterranean Air Command.
MEHQ	Middle East Command Headquarters.
MMG	Medium Machine Gun.
MOD	Ministry of Defence.
MTB	Motor Torpedo Boat.
NCO	Non-Commissioned Officer.
OKW	Oberkommando der Wehrmacht.
OP	Observation Post.
PM	Prime Minister.
PR	Photographic Reconnaissance.
RA	Royal Artillery.
RE	Royal Engineers.
RHA	Royal Horse Artillery.
RIF	Royal Irish Fusiliers.
RWK	Royal West Kent Regiment.

SAS	Special Air Service Regiment.
SBS	Special Boat Service.
SBNO	Senior British Naval Officer.
SIGINT	Signals Intelligence.
USJCOS	United States Joint Chiefs of Staff.
VCNS	Vice Chief Naval Staff (British).
VCOS	Vice Chiefs of Staff (British).
VHF	Very High Frequency.

Code Names

ACCOLADE	Allied Operations in the Aegean.
ANVIL	Allied Landings in Southern France.
AVALANCHE	Allied Landings at Salerno.
BARBAROSSA	German Invasion of Russia.
BAYTOWN	Allied Landings at Reggio di Calabria.
BULLFROG	Allied Operations in the Arakan.
COCKADE	Cover and Deception, Western Europe.
DRAGOON	Replaced "Anvil."
EUREKA	Teheran Conference, November 1943.
FREEDOM	General Eisenhower.
HANDCUFF	Allied Operations to Capture Rhodes.
HARDIHOOD	Allied Assistance to Turkey.
HERCULES	Replaced "Handcuff."
HUSKY	Allied Landings in Sicily.
LEOPARD	German Attack against Leros.
MINCEMEAT	Cover and Deception, Mediterranean 1943.
OVERLORD	Cross-Channel Invasion.
POINTBLANK	Allied Strategic Air Plan.
PRICELESS	Operations in the Mediterranean.
QUADRANT	First Quebec Conference, August 1943.
SATURN	Replaced "Hardihood."
SEXTANT	Cairo Conference, November-December 1943.
SHINGLE	Allied Landings at Anzio.
SYMBOL	Casablanca Conference, January 1943.
TORCH	Allied Landings in North Africa.
TRIDENT	Third Washington Conference, May 1943.
ZEPPELIN	Cover and Deception, Balkans 1943.

Part I
Strategic Objectives

Introduction

This is a story about amphibious operations in the Aegean Sea during World War II. It is not a history, per se, rather, it is an account designed to explore, interpret, and reassess the crucial decisions which influenced the outcome of what has become known as the "Dodecanese Disaster." British operations in the Aegean present some parallels in scale and order of battle with the recent conflict in the Falklands, the critical difference being that, in the case of the Aegean, the reach of politicians and planners exceeded their grasp. As a consequence, the task force failed to achieve its objectives and as always, luck was the residue of design.

By September 1943, German forces had been cleared from North Africa, the siege of Malta had been lifted, Sicily was in Allied hands and our forces were invading the Italian Peninsula. Moreover, the Allies had at their disposal in the Mediterranean theatre 4,000 warplanes against a Luftwaffe strength of 850 planes of all types, only 500 of which were serviceable. The war's center of gravity had shifted from Cairo to Algiers, and the Americans were assuming command.

Operations in the Dodecanese Islands were planned originally as a preliminary step toward bringing Turkey into the War on the Allied side. When Italy surrendered in September 1943, the Aegean venture was designed by the British to exploit the surrender to the fullest extent. The Mission was conceived as an amphibious operation under the code name ACCOLADE, to capture Rhodes, and to walk in and hold some of the smaller islands in the Aegean which, at the time, were not occupied by the Germans.

The objectives were to carry out a piratical war on enemy communications in the Aegean; covertly, to induce Turkey to enter the War on the Allied side; to stimulate partisan movements in Yugoslavia and Greece; and to weaken the German hold over the Balkans. Other benefits, it was said, would be to divert German forces from the Italian front during the critical days covering the Salerno landings.

The Mission was remarkable for its bold conception. Indeed, for a fleeting moment it seemed just possible that a lodgment in the Dodecanese might be successful. However, the prospect was soon obliterated by a succession of setbacks that, on their face, were inevitable. President Franklin Roosevelt, to whom Prime Minister Winston Churchill deferred, and General Dwight Eisenhower as Supreme Commander both perceived the Aegean operations as an adventure that was, "highly prejudicial to the success of Italian operations and likely to impinge on longer term planning for OVERLORD."(1)

Roosevelt, Eisenhower, and the US Chiefs of Staff considered any major expedition into the Aegean to be the thin end of the wedge. It would likely induce a growing commitment for men and materiel, detracting in no small measure from the main effort against the Nazi power, plans for which had been drawn up by the Joint Chiefs of Staff. The Americans distrusted Churchill, "as a man who liked 'exotic' operations and who also went back on agreements he had accepted."(2)

How far were the Americans willing to support an Aegean venture? In Washington, the USJCOS directed their planning staff to consider actions that might follow the Allied invasion of Sicily. Forrest C. Pogue, General George C. Marshall's biographer, writes:

> General Marshall instructed Eisenhower to draft plans for a full scale invasion of Italy and an offensive effort in the direction of Crete and the Dodecanese Islands with the object of encouraging Turkey to enter the war on the side of the Allies--recommendations that Marshall expected the Prime Minister to make. It was, however, only an exercise. "You will understand that the operations outlined above are not in keeping with my ideas of what our strategy should be. The decisive effort must be made against the Continent from the United Kingdom."(3)

From the American point of view, the campaign in the Mediterranean reflected a British preoccupation with the Middle East and with the protection and ultimate enhancement of their interests in that region. The British strategy was to draw German formations into southern Italy, thus reducing the enemy's potential strength in western Europe. As the Allied campaign in Sicily moved toward certain success, the Americans agreed to a plan to invest the Italian Peninsula, an undertaking that proved costly for the Allies, particularly for the American divisions involved.

General Marshall's reference to the Dodecanese and to Turkey was to throw Churchill a bone. However, as German resistance in Italy stiffened and the prospect for a war of attrition became more apparent, American tolerance for British adventures in the eastern Mediterranean quickly evaporated.

The British Prime Minister, however, never allowed his concern for the Italian front to overshadow his determination to mount operations in the Aegean. Marshall's instructions to Eisenhower, which tacitly at least recognized the prospect for operations in support of Turkey, were regarded by Churchill as a sign of accord, indeed as a benediction for a thrust into the Balkans. The collapse of Mussolini served to strengthen the Prime Minister's resolve.

Churchill's extraordinary efforts to co-opt Roosevelt and Eisenhower in support of his objectives in the eastern Mediterranean, and the Americans' resistance to the Prime Minister's ambitious but ill-conceived plans, stem from Churchill's interpretation of Marshall's earlier instructions to the Allied Commander. However, as the fighting on the Italian front increased in intensity, Churchill's demands on Eisenhower to support the Aegean enterprise came to be resented, by both American and British commanders.

The British had a four-point plan, which was to become operational should Turkey elect to enter the War. A desirable condition of the plan was for the British to secure the island of Rhodes. On 9-10 September, Major The Earl Jellicoe, SBS, accompanied by Major Dalby and Sergeant Kesterton parachuted onto Rhodes in the hope of persuading the Italian Governor, Admiral Campioni, to use his 30,000-strong garrison in support of a British attempt to capture the island, but the Germans immediately seized the initiative, and the chance was lost.

Seven plans for capturing the key island of Rhodes and the smaller islands of Kos and Leros were put forward. All came to nothing. The island of Kos was attacked by a German battle group on 3 October and fell within twenty-four hours after a weak defense, which the British Prime Minister described as, "an unsatisfactory resistance."(4) Ten days before Leros was assaulted by German amphibious forces on 12 November, Churchill remarked: "We are very near a most vexatious disaster in this part of the world."(5)

Having warmed up on Kos, the German battle group proceeded to redeploy their Kos task force against Leros, with two parachute regiments providing the cutting edge for the assault. When the island fell after five days of intensive fighting, Churchill said: "Leros fell after an unexpectedly prolonged resistance."(6)

The British garrison on Leros had comprised three, and by the last day, four infantry battalions. Static troops, jaded from three years on Malta: "They fought doggedly and without success."(7) Squadrons of the elite Long Range Desert Group and the Special Boat Service were mauled, while the Royal Navy suffered appalling losses; one-third of the entire Mediterranean fleet was sunk or crippled.

Were the Aegean operations sound in concept, plan, and execution? If not, were the Allies at risk due to faulty strategy, poor planning, or inadequate defense? In attempting to answer these provocative questions there were, at the time, a number of turning points for decision making in the Aegean:

* Up to the surrender of Italy (18 July-9 Sept)
* Up to the attack on Kos (10 Sept-3 Oct)
* Up to the La Marsa conference (4 Oct-10 Oct)
* Up to the acceptance of the Foreign Secretary's recommendations from Cairo (11 Oct-14 Oct)
* Up to the attack on Leros (15 Oct-12 Nov).

This book traces the fateful attempts made by the British, in the face of strong opposition from President Roosevelt, General Eisenhower, and other commanders, to mount offensive operations in the Aegean in September 1943. The story illustrates the tension between the Allies, at both the political and military levels, in advocating and establishing strategic objectives and priorities leading to the commitment of Allied forces in the eastern Mediterranean.

It is hoped that this account will serve as a tribute to those who were cut down on the rocky slopes of the islands, who perished in the sea, or who were blown out of the sky; men who, as Brigadier CJC Molony remarked, "deserved their laurels won not by victory but by their faithful obedience to orders."(8) This book is not concerned with platitudes; it offers little comfort, except that which comes from understanding the hard truth.

NOTES

1. Public Record Office, London, WO 106/3152, General Dwight D. Eisenhower.

2. Elisabeth Barker, Churchill and Eden at War (London: Macmillan, 1978), 134.

3. Forrest C. Pogue, George C. Marshall: Organizer of Victory, 1943-1945 (New York: Viking Press, 1973), 194.

4. Public Record Office, London, PREM 3/3/5, Winston S. Churchill.

5. Ibid.

6. Ibid.

7. CJC Molony et al., The Mediterranean and Middle East, vol. 5, History of the Second World War (London: Her Majesty's Stationery Office, 1973), 557.

8. Ibid., 559.

The Dodecanese: Geo-Political Profile

The Dodecanese, also known as the Southern Sporades, is a group of twelve islands, lying off the south-west coast of Anatolia. The group consists of the islands of Patmos, Lipsos, Levita, Leros, Kalymnos, Kos, Nisyros, Piscopi, Simi, Chalkia, Stampalia, and Casos, together with Scarpanto, Rhodes, and Kastellorizo.(1) Geological evidence shows that the islands once formed part of the Anatolian mainland. Only now in a more recent geomorphological era do they appear as the peaks of underwater mountains.

The first steps toward European civilization were taken in the insular and peninsular lands between the Ionian and Aegean Seas. Our earliest picture comes from the Homeric catalogue between 1500 and 1000 B.C., when the Mediterranean was colonized by Greece and the Greek colonies. Rhodes was then a center of overseas trade for the three towns of Kamiros, Lindos, and Ialysos until their inhabitants built the city of Rhodes in 407 B.C. The island was occupied by the Greeks until the end of the Seventh Century, when it passed to the Saracens. At the beginning of the Eleventh Century, Rhodes was still within the Byzantine Empire as a link to the Mediterranean trade route. During the Thirteenth Century the Venetians seized all the islands along the trade route which it then monopolized.

Rhodes and the islands of the Dodecanese were occupied by the Knights of St John from the early Fourteenth Century until 1522, when the Sultan, Suliman the Magnificent, evicted the Knights after a stubborn siege. The Sultan raised the Ottoman Empire to the heights of its glory, and the islands remained under Turkish rule for a period of 400 years, until the Italo-Turkish War in 1912. In May of that year, an Italian force took possession of Rhodes, while simultaneously landing on the other islands. The first Treaty of Lausanne, which ended the Libyan War, left the islands in the hands of the Italians.

During the Italian occupation, the islanders suffered from political as well as economic disadvantages. At the same time, the Italians did much to improve the quality of life on the islands by introducing schools, hospitals, and public works and bringing the benefits of settled government. Although of Greek origin, the inhabitants were Italian citizens. However, they were not allowed to vote although Italy was prepared to concede this point if the islanders were willing to accept the obligation of military service. Communication with the mainland was restricted, and the island of Leros became a prohibited area for everyone except Italian military personnel.

Throughout the Italian occupation, many islanders held Pan-Hellenic ideals, and the Orthodox Church remained the center of sentiment for union with Greece. The Italians were always mindful of the strategic importance of the islands in the eastern Mediterranean, as bases for operations against the mainland. Between 1935 and 1940, they developed an air base on Rhodes and an airfield on Kos. Leros was equipped with a seaplane base, but in those days, there was no landing strip on the island.

Prior to the outbreak of World War II on the 3 September 1939, the British were engaged in intelligence gathering in the Aegean. Detailed reports were prepared on the history and geo-political significance of the Dodecanese Islands under the Knights of St John, Turkish rule, and the Italian occupation, followed by an appreciation of Italy's Mediterranean policy in the period leading up to World War II. These reports also described the system of government on the islands.

Defense inventories were taken of all naval and military installations, barbed wire systems, searchlight and gun emplacements, fuel tanks, barracks, harbor installations, airfields, wireless telegraphy stations and telephone systems, submarine cables, miscellaneous stores, water supply reservoirs, and the state of roads. All gun positions and other significant details were recorded in degrees of longitude and latitude. The elaborate survey was conducted on an island-by-island basis.(2)

During the war, British Prime Minister Winston Churchill first used British troops to occupy some of the islands and then supported a plan for the Turkish Army to capture Rhodes and the Dodecanese, at the time occupied by the Germans. Shortly after the end of World War II, Rhodes and the Dodecanese were ceded to Greece under whose sovereignty they remain. In the long post-war period since then, Turkey has continued to exert pressure on Greece with respect to hegemony over the islands and the off-shore sea bed of the Aegean, which undoubtedly contains rich deposits of oil and natural gas.(3)

NOTES

1.   In The Aegean Mission, the author has used the Greek transliteration for Kos, Kalymnos, and Kastellorizo.

2.   Public Record Office, London, WO 208/689.

3.   Author's   Note: In   a   note   on   page   539   of   The
Mediterranean and Middle East, vol. 5, CJC Molony says: "The
Prime Minister's belief that Leros was a fortified naval base
with powerful permanent batteries could not have been derived
from the information at his disposal." From the evidence in WO
208/689,   it   would   appear   to   the   contrary   that,   the   Prime
Minister   was   in   possession   of   a   wealth   of   detail   on   the
defensive   installations   on   Rhodes,   Leros,   and   all   the   other
islands of the Dodecanese.

Anglo-American Attitudes

The inability of British forces to capture and hold islands in the Aegean in the autumn of 1943 can be attributed to two principal causes: first, the failure of the Americans to provide logistical support in furtherance of a British policy with which, in principle, they were opposed; and second, the protracted British insistence that operations should continue long after all logic suggested that they ought to be abandoned. Thus, the twin horns of the dilemma posed both strategic and tactical problems, which soon polarized Allied plans for operations in the Mediterranean.

Both the Americans and the British argued from divergent viewpoints that there were, indeed, far reaching implications and consequences attendant upon operations in the eastern Mediterranean, which, by extension, were perceived as a precursor to an Allied commitment in the Balkans. The Americans felt strongly that the Aegean option implied a departure from agreed plans. These plans would be impacted by siphoning off resources already allocated for operations in the central Mediterranean and northwestern Europe. Mark Stoler comments on the conclusions reached at the Casablanca Conference code-named SYMBOL: "At the 18 January meeting, Churchill requested inclusion of clauses in the final Combined Chiefs of Staff (CCS) document giving the British a 'free hand' to deal with the Turks and mentioning the possibility of operations in the Dodecanese."(1)

The agreed strategy, stemming from the Casablanca Conference in January 1943 and the Washington Conference in May 1943, was to plan for a cross-Channel invasion in May 1944, and, in the interim, to clear the Germans out of Tunisia followed by an assault on Sicily. Subsequently, agreement was reached to invest the Italian Peninsula with landings at Reggio di Calabria and then at Salerno. Meanwhile, a plan to mount operations in the south of France was designed to keep the Germans guessing as to Allied intentions. During this period, the Balkans option was argued fiercely between the Americans and the British in the context of an overall Mediterranean strategy.

In The Politics of the Second Front, Stoler outlines the perceived problem of when and where to open the front and the constant pressure by the Russians for action by the Western Powers. Stoler comments: "In total, the military decisions of the Casablanca conference were highly political."(2) Churchill's fixation on Turkey, tacitly agreed upon with Roosevelt and Marshall, served if nothing else, to enhance the perceived value of Allied operations in the Mediterranean, and thus, also served to appease the Russians, at least for the time being.

Anticipating the collapse of Italy, the British felt that new opportunities would present themselves in the eastern Mediterranean. These would include the ability of the Allies to render assistance to partisan movements in Yugoslavia and Greece, to bring about the capture of Rhodes and other islands in the Dodecanese and, with control over the Aegean, to secure a passage through the Dardanelles and the Black Sea for convoys to Russia. The prime strategic benefit would be the likely decision by Turkey to enter the War, thus bringing to bear the weight of its forty-six divisions in support of the Allied cause.

To achieve these ends, the British had prepared two plans: ACCOLADE for the capture of Crete, Rhodes, and other islands, to be followed by HARDIHOOD, a four-point plan of logistical support for military aid to Turkey. This aid was to include fifty squadrons of fighter planes, ten AA regiments, five anti-tank regiments, and two armored divisions. Post-war realignments would see the Dodecanese ceded to Turkey.

The positions that the Americans and the British took by August 1943 had become diametrically opposed. Churchill dismissed the concerns expressed by President Roosevelt, General Eisenhower, and indeed, by some British commanders who were firmly against operations in the Aegean. Presumably the Prime Minister's vision had some strategic merit, but so also did the plans previously formulated by the Joint Planners and agreed upon by the British Chiefs of Staff (COS), the US Joint Chiefs of Staff (USJCOS), and the Combined Chiefs of Staff (CCS). However, at no time was a Balkans Plan put forward as an agreed alternative to OVERLORD or AVALANCHE to be weighed in the balancing of strategic objectives.

The Aegean option, advocated by the British, was always based on nothing more than expedient provisions to induce Turkey to enter the war. Churchill saw the surrender of Italy as an opportune moment to play the Turkish card. Of Churchill it has been said that, "he did in fact fear a repetition of the senseless slaughter of the Western Front offensives of the First World War."(3) A well-known historian places a fine point on this observation: "He merely retained his illusion, over thirty years old, that there was somewhere an easy backdoor into Germany, and hoped to win the war by some unexpected miracle instead of by heavy fighting."(4)

Of necessity if not by choice, Churchill was willing to accept heavy casualties elsewhere. Max Hastings comments: "Over 55,000 Commonwealth aircrew were killed in Bomber Command alone, more than the British Army's total loss of officers in World War I."(5) What is more important to examine than a single emotive causality is the objective behind the Prime Minister's perceptive judgment, that the Turkish hand was indeed the one to play. Part of the problem lies in the Prime Minister's evasiveness: "There has never been any question of major action in the Balkans."(6) It will become clear that Churchill is being disingenuous on this point.

Contingency planning for ACCOLADE shows that, from carefully drawn plans using three infantry divisions and supporting arms, a commitment was finally made to defend three small islands with a single British infantry brigade, without having first captured the key objective, the island of Rhodes. As a consequence the broader strategic objective of bringing Turkey into the War was flawed from the outset.

The first island to be attacked by the Germans was Kos. It fell on 3 October, within twenty-four hours of the initial assault. Six weeks later the second island, Leros, fell. The third island, Samos, was evacuated, but not before its infantry garrison was thrown in on the last days of the action to support the troops on Leros.

The Prime Minister expressed regret, if not remorse, over these events. Others sought to justify the diversionary effects of the Aegean action on the German formations, otherwise able to concentrate on the Italian front. Meanwhile, many British commanders pointed to the sheer folly of trying to carry out combined operations without air cover, resulting in prohibitive naval losses. Professor FH Hinsley writes:

> SW Roskill, the official British historian of the war at sea, after criticizing the decision to embark on the Aegean operations in the knowledge that Rhodes could not be captured, was still more critical of the decision to continue with them when it had become clear that we could not exercise adequate maritime control over the disputed waters--and this unpleasant fact was abundantly plain after the fall of Kos on 3 October, if not earlier.(7)

Luftwaffe air squadrons maintained dominance over the Aegean throughout the entire operation and the GAF extracted a costly price from the Royal Navy, in its attempts to sustain the British force which had been sent up to the islands.

In order to understand the tangible benefits which may have resulted from British actions in the Aegean following the abdication of Mussolini on 25 July 1943, it is necessary to comprehend the way in which the surrender of Italy was conducted. In the interim period between 25 July and 3 September, the Armistice was secretly signed in Syracuse, and on 8 September, the Badoglio Government publicly asked for an armistice. On the following day, forty-six days after the fall of Mussolini, Allied forces landed at Salerno.

In this six-week interval, the Germans had not been idle. As early as 29 July, German forces had occupied Trieste, Pola, Fiume, the Istrian Peninsula, and the Udine. Meanwhile, German divisions in the Balkans had been increased from eight divisions in March to eighteen by 10 July. Allied strategy for operations in the Mediterranean should have been carefully prepared with the Badoglio group well in advance of Mussolini's overthrow, not simply as a reaction to the coup d'etat.

The Middle East Headquarters responded quickly, but only after the event, with a three-man mission to Rhodes, on 9 and 10 September. To suppose that these envoys could turn the Italian garrison around remains the supreme folly simply because there was no Allied force available to effect the capture of the island.

The Joint Planners discounted any prospect of an Allied assault on Crete. British Commonwealth forces had already lost 1,545 men in earlier battles for possession of the island. With respect to the Aegean, it was not going to be simply a matter of giving the Italians assistance in rounding up the German garrisons. The Germans would fight, and there would be a heavy commitment in servicing amphibious operations.

The Americans looked long and hard at the implications of supporting the Aegean option. They were concerned not only with the first step, but with subsequent events, and the consequences that might follow. The Greeks, for example, did not take kindly to the status of co-belligerent recently accorded to the much hated Italians, while the Romanians and the Turks were wary of Russian intentions. Meanwhile, of major concern to the Allied commanders in the central Mediterranean, the Germans were at the point of decision to fight a major battle south of Rome.

From the most fundamental expression of Allied strategy to the smaller yet significant detail of logistical support for the units soon to be engaged in fighting for the Dodecanese, the Anglo-American position remained at variance. Against an estimated build up of some twenty-two German divisions, the Allies were assembling in Italy a mixed force of eleven divisions comprising American, British, Canadian, New Zealand, Indian, and Polish formations. By diverting resources to the eastern Mediterranean, the Allies would be running an increased risk of a setback in northern Italy.

Within the British command there was confusion as to aims, purposes and timing. The CIGS Sir Alan Brooke said that, "there was a grave danger that we should find ourselves being drawn into an amphibious campaign in the eastern Mediterranean which would absorb resources which might be badly needed in Italy."(8)

One month later the CIGS took the opposite view:

> When I look at the Mediterranean, I realize only
> too well how far I have failed. If only I had
> sufficient force of character to swing those
> American Chiefs of Staff around and make them see
> daylight, how different the war might be. We
> should have the whole Balkans ablaze by now, and
> the war might have been finished in 1943.(9)

Such diametrically opposed viewpoints indicate indecision on
the part of the CIGS as to the best course of action to follow.
His opinion may well have been influenced by others, since Brooke
also attributes the expression "Balkans ablaze" to Churchill.
This irresolute attitude, which firmed up only after the success
of OVERLORD, is indicative of the sharp divisions that pervaded
the Allied Command structure at the time. Moreover, it is
distressing to read how a man in Brooke's position could have
been so indecisive.

Yugoslavia was in a turmoil; the pot that boiled contained the
elements of both ethnic and political instability. The Greeks,
no less, were fractured by a power struggle between rival
partisan factions of varying political hue. Compounded by
Bulgarian, Romanian, and Turkish tensions, with the omnipotent
presence of the Soviet Union (with its borders on Turkey, Persia,
and Afghanistan), not only might the Balkans be ablaze, but the
Middle East also.

In light of the meticulous planning for operations in France
and Germany, it is difficult to understand why the British should
be fascinated by the "soft underbelly" approach. There never
was a soft underbelly; rather a tortuous tangent, beset with
formidable physical obstacles and intractable animosities. The
Americans were wise not to fall for what would have become a war
of attrition in the Balkans.

The Balkans, a mountainous, undeveloped region with primitive
roads, was always volatile, with nests of intrigue and feuding
factions. At no time did the Balkan states evidence antipathy
toward the Germans greater than that which they felt for one
another. For many in the Balkans, in the Levant, and in the
Middle East, Germany was not an enemy at all. With countries
such as Romania and Hungary, Germany was formally allied, while
with others, she remained affectively neutral; none more so than
with Turkey.

The sphere of influence of the Balkans is some 1,500 miles
distant from the heartland of Europe (Istanbul to Paris). The
bitter struggle for the Italian Peninsula, which was part of the
so-called "soft underbelly" of Europe, provides an example of
the attrition that Allied forces would have confronted in the
Balkans. It took eight months for the Allies to advance only
one hundred miles from Naples to Rome. Alan Brooke's dream of a
Balkans venture would have become a nightmare for the Allies.

At the very least, it would have given Germany a respite from massing divisions on its western approaches, and in 1943, the Germans were not yet mortally weakened by the Russian Army.

A series of guerrilla actions would have ensued. Battles in the Balkans would have done little to shift the strategic center of the war from western Europe. The American commitment that the British COS had obtained, to limit the war against Japan in favor of Mediterranean operations, would have been jeopardized. Moreover, the British would have become bogged down in a peripheral action that was politically volatile and militarily of marginal value. Churchill, of course, was concerned with securing the periphery to the Middle East oil-bearing region and with denying Russia access to the Dardanelles.

Had there been a measure of military success for Allied operations in the Balkans, it could only have been achieved with the acquiescence and support of the Russians. The post-war situation would, therefore, have found a far stronger Soviet presence in the Balkans, the Levant, and the Middle East than that which actually transpired. In addition to the central European states coming within the Soviet sphere of influence (and by extension, control), Stalin could also then lay claim to the Balkans, the Levant, Afghanistan, and ultimately Iran, Iraq, and the Arabian Peninsula.

If this scenario can be accepted, it goes some way to explaining why the Americans were totally opposed to taking on obligations in the Balkans. From the American perspective, a Balkans bridgehead would not strike at the heart of Nazi Germany and thus would weaken rather than strengthen the ability of the Allies to take the pressure off Russian forces. The Americans were most wary of the synergistic effects that a Balkans campaign would have had on the prosecution of the war, and they may have been aware of the potential political aftermath. In any event, arguments in support of an Aegean option, appeared to the Americans to generate more heat than light.

After the fall of Kos, President Roosevelt remarked: "Strategically if we get the Aegean Islands, I ask myself where do we go from there, and vice versa, where would the Germans go if for some time they retain possession of the islands?"(10) However, the final decision was left to General Eisenhower. Churchill's staff officer, General Sir Hastings Ismay, said: "The Prime Minister thought he would change his mind, and instructed us to do all in our power to persuade him to do so."(11) This attempt to exert such undue influence on the Allied Military Commander and by extension, on General Marshall and President Roosevelt clearly demonstrates that Winston Churchill was intent on much more than the possession of a few small islands.

Churchill's notion was to sponsor an offensive in the Balkans, if necessary at the expense of OVERLORD. The fact that the Prime Minister hoped to use forty-six Turkish divisions rather than British forces as cannon fodder is not disputed. Winston

Churchill was an opportunist, and with the surrender of Italy he spotted what he thought was an opportunity to press for the Turkish option. While Field Marshal Jan Smuts was also an exponent of a Balkans strategy, most British commanders were opposed.

Professor Erhman has written that: "A week before the conference at Cairo began, Marshall told Roosevelt and Hopkins, at a meeting of the Joint Chiefs of Staff, that the British might like to 'ditch' OVERLORD now in order to go into the Balkans."(12) Given the need for a strong coalition in planning for the Normandy invasion, Marshall's warning, if of substance, suggests a reckless intent on the part of the British Prime Minister. The historical evidence supports Marshall's concern.

Whatever his motives, Churchill did his best to leapfrog over agreed Allied plans and strategies. The strategy of the Prime Minister with respect to the Balkans is minuted on three separate occasions: to the COS Committee on 19 October 1943; to the COS on "Future Operations in the European and Mediterranean Theatres," 20 November 1943; and at the Conference of Dominions' Prime Ministers in London in May 1944. At the conference in London on 3 May, Churchill is reported as saying that:

> He was bound to admit that if he had had his own way, the layout of the war would have been different. His inclination would have been in favor of rolling up Europe from the southeast, and joining hands with the Russians. However, it had proved impossible to persuade the United States on this view. They had been determined at every stage upon the invasion of northwest Europe. He himself had opposed the opening of this campaign in 1942 and 1943, but was now in favor of it, and all his military advisers supported him in this. Russian pressure, too, had been very severe. Meanwhile, in Italy we must strike and prevent the enemy drawing his forces away.(13)

Later in the same meeting, Churchill again confirmed that there had never been any question of major action in the Balkans. It was merely a question of assistance by commandos and air actions. To the contrary, the British plan for HARDIHOOD suggests that the Prime Minister was intent on committing major Allied forces to the Balkans. He undoubtedly was also concerned to block any secret protocols which would bring Russia within range of the Bosphorus, enhancing present and future Soviet geo-political aspirations in the region. His stated purpose, however, was to assist the Russians.

In an appreciation of the events in the Dodecanese, a military analyst, Major-General Rowan-Robinson, felt that this action in the islands had proved to be a misfortune for the Allies:

> They were on a small scale, indeed, but they left
> a definite blot on the brilliant strategy which
> we had pursued in the Mediterranean during the
> past year. It is curious, indeed, that geography
> should have been ignored for, of all the
> innumerable factors that can make or mar a plan,
> it is the only one that is truly stable. It is
> to be hoped that when the full facts are known,
> these criticisms of our strategy will prove to be
> of a superficial nature and also some better
> reason will be advanced for our action than that
> of a natural reluctance to abandon conquered
> territory. A final point, our experience in the
> Dodecanese shows the successful defense of Malta
> to have been little short of miraculous.(14)

Once the Italians on Rhodes had capitulated to the Germans there appeared to be only one course for General Wilson to follow, namely to evacuate the captured islands. Instead the British hung on, and even after the surrender of Kos had rendered the other islands still less tenable they actually reinforced Leros, thus largely increasing the number of troops bound to be captured there. Only after the loss of Leros did the British abandon Samos.

Official reports, many unpublished, on ACCOLADE and on HARDIHOOD, form the basis of this story. From the official record and from informed comment by Allied commanders, the reader can draw conclusions as to the truth behind British intentions and American concerns with respect to the Dodecanese theatre of operations. Churchill was a force to be reckoned with; exercising dictatorial power over his subordinate Generals and not inconsiderable influence with the President of the United States. It is against these perceptions of Allied strategy that the Aegean venture must be evaluated.

NOTES

1.   Mark A. Stoler, The Politics of the Second Front (Westport, Connecticut: Greenwood Press, 1977), 76.

2.   Ibid., 78.

3.   Peter Smith and Edwin Walker, War in the Aegean (London: William Kimber, 1974), 49.

4.   AJP Taylor, English History, 1914-1945 (Oxford: Oxford University Press, 1965), 573.

5.   Max Hastings, Bomber Command (London: Michael Joseph, 1979), 9.

6.   John Erhman, Grand Strategy, vol. 5, History of the Second World War (London: Her Majesty's Stationery Office, 1956), 555.

7.   FH Hinsley, British Intelligence in the Second World War, vol. 3, part 1 (Cambridge: Cambridge University Press, 1979), 149.

8.   Public Record Office, London, PREM 3/3/5, General Sir Alan Brooke.

9.   Sir Arthur Bryant, Triumph in the West (New York: Doubleday, 1959), 37.

10.   CJC Molony et al., The Mediterranean and Middle East, vol. 5, History of the Second World War (London: Her Majesty's Stationery Office, 1973), 545.

11.   Lord Ismay, The Memoirs of General Lord Ismay (London: William Heinemann, 1960), 323.

12.   Erhman, Grand Strategy, 117.

13.   Ibid., 555.

14.   Major-General H. Rowan-Robinson, The Surrender of Italy (London: RUSI Journal, November 1943), 273.

Strategy: Straws in the Wind

Allied plans for operations in all theatres of war decided the disposition of manpower, shipping, and other resources to the battlefronts. For the most part, Allied planning was highly successful. However, as may be expected, it was sometimes necessary to depart from a set plan, to improvise, and to take risks.

Faced with so few resources in the early days of the War, the British were more inclined to improvise than were the Americans who were strong on organization, procurement of materiel and master planning. Having set objectives and priorities, the Americans were not impressed with ad hoc decisions, least of all with actions likely to impair the implementation of carefully laid plans.

Throughout, the Americans remained highly skeptical of British initiatives that were concerned primarily with operations in the eastern Mediterranean. Even more important, the Americans believed that a Balkans approach was thoroughly unsound strategy. Eisenhower was more inclined to listen to the advice of General George C. Marshall, Chairman of the US Joint Chiefs of Staff, than to the exhortations of the British Prime Minister. Throughout, the Americans felt closely bound by the agreements reached at successive Allied conferences.

Strategic planning for the war in Europe was agreed upon at Casablanca in January 1943, at Washington in May 1943, and at Quebec in August of the same year. At Casablanca, the Allies identified the primary objective: to plan for a cross-Channel invasion, under the code name OVERLORD, designed to take place in May 1944. Policy with respect to operations in the Mediterranean was initially limited to an assault against Sicily under the code name HUSKY. Subsequent operations in the Mediterranean under the code name PRICELESS would be determined in light of circumstances following HUSKY.

The decision was then made to invest the Italian mainland with two offensive actions to be carried out by the American Fifth Army and the British Eighth Army. With landings at Reggio di Calabria, the initial assault, under the code name BAYTOWN, took place on 3 September, four years to the day after Britain had declared war on Germany. On 9 September, the Allies attacked at Salerno with operation AVALANCHE. The capture of Corsica and Sardinia was to be incidental to operations against the Italian Peninsula, if circumstances warranted such further ventures.

OVERLORD would be the primary Allied ground and air effort against the Axis Powers in Europe. Because of the rival claims of the Normandy landings and the Mediterranean theatre, the allocation of scarce resources would be made with the main object of ensuring the success of OVERLORD and, according to Molony, "the strategic concept never changed."(1) All the plans competed for scarce resources.

Meanwhile, no one could decide which operational plan or combination of plans would be used because the problem of invading the Italian mainland or the Mediterranean islands, "bristled with unknowns to which on-going events alone could give values."(2) Given this uncertainty, the consequences of deviating from a preferred course of action had to be constantly reassessed and redefined.

To place the Aegean sphere of operations in perspective, it is first necessary to identify plans made in the early months of the War as well as those which emerged later. TRIDENT confirmed the overall strategic concept for the prosecution of the War. In respect to the Mediterranean theatre, Eisenhower was instructed to plan such operations as would be best calculated to eliminate Italy from the war and to contain the greatest number of German forces. The Combined Chiefs of Staff (CCS) would decide which of these operations were to be adopted and prepared.

QUADRANT reaffirmed the overall strategic concept. The approved plans and operations were: first, the elimination of Italy as a belligerent; second, the seizure of Corsica and Sardinia; third, unremitting pressure on German forces in northern Italy. The Allied Chiefs agreed: "Operations in the Balkans area were to be limited to the supply of Balkan guerrillas, by air and sea transport, to minor commando forces and to the bombing of strategic objectives."(3) Rhodes was the key to these operations. Stoler says: "Once again, Churchill was not being honest, and the American planners were quite correct in assessing his political motives for such an attack."(4) The Prime Minister intended to go farther into the Balkans, with Turkey as the beachhead.

An important strategic objective in the Mediterranean theatre was the Aegean Sea: "An area which the British had long wished to control, without having the necessary means."(5) With the Aegean in Allied hands, the British felt that Turkey would probably come into the war and convoys could then be sent to Russia via the Dardanelles and the Black Sea. The prime mover in this strategy was Winston Churchill. His staff officer, Lieutenant-General Sir Hastings Ismay, records: "Churchill's underlying object was in fact much the same as that which had inspired him in 1915. To accomplish these ends it was deemed necessary to first capture Rhodes and possibly other islands in the Dodecanese."(6) Ismay's reference is, of course, to the disastrous Gallipoli Campaign in World War I.

THE AEGEAN 1940-1941

In 1940-1941, the Italians continued to provide military garrisons for the Dodecanese Islands as they had from 1912 onward. These islands were clearly of strategic importance to the security of the Italian Empire in northeast Africa. Similarly, the British were concerned about the control of shipping in the Mediterranean and the further implications for the protection of Malta, the Suez Canal, and the Red Sea route to India. All these areas were threatened by the Italian occupation of Ethiopia, Eritrea, Libya, and Somaliland. When Italy entered the War on 10 June 1940, the importance of the Dodecanese, Rhodes, and Crete became even more critical to British strategy.

Early in 1940, British naval and military planners put forward proposals to conduct night raids on the smaller islands in the Dodecanese, to dismay the Italians and encourage the Greeks and Turks. There was much discussion on the subject of possible raids into the Aegean in 1940. However, "it was quickly decided that Rhodes was too difficult to tackle."(7) A significant statement on the question of mounting an attack in the Dodecanese was made by Churchill as early as 13 January 1941. The PM minuted General Ismay:

> I do not think that it would be wise to attack these small islands. They are no use in themselves, they are not necessary for the attack on the larger islands. Now that we hold Crete, stirring up this quarter will put the enemy on their guard, and will bring about the disagreement between Greece and Turkey which has become only too apparent as we have explored tentatively this subject. The Defense Committee has not approved these operations.(8)

Ignoring his own note of caution, Churchill, in January 1941, sent No. Fiftieth Commando on a reconnaissance to Crete, and on 24 February, as a raiding force to Kastellorizo. The Italians seized the initiative and this small British force had to withdraw; a small scale SNAFU.

In October 1940, Mussolini launched an attack on Greece. Although Greece had earlier received a British guarantee of support, the Greeks held their own and did not invoke British aid for fear of provoking a German response. Following the success of Wavell's victories against Mussolini's troops in Libya, Hitler despatched the Afrika Korps to the Western Desert and prepared to attack Greece. Turkey looked on. The British, even with their resources fully stretched in Libya, were aware of German preparations to attack in Greece.

In March 1941, the British withdrew a force of 62,000 men from the Middle East to meet the anticipated German attack on Greece. The Germans invaded in April 1941. The inferior British force never came to grips with the enemy; 50,000 were taken off, having lost most of their equipment; most were evacuated to the island of Crete and back to their bases in the Middle East. On 20 May, General Student's Eleventh Air Corps--which included a parachute division, a glider regiment, an Alpine division, and tank units, invaded Crete. After ten days of fierce fighting the bulk of the British force was evacuated, leaving 8,000 troops to fall into captivity. Neither the Turks nor the Russians lifted a finger to help the Greeks.

By the early summer of 1941, the British had been thrown out of Greece and Crete, the Germans were rapidly taking over from the Italians in Libya, while Greece and the Balkans were heavily invested by Axis troops. Turkey, the sworn enemy of Greece, prudently decided to maintain her neutrality, with a bias toward the German cause. On the eve of BARBAROSSA, Turkey signed a ten year treaty with Germany. David Irving records: ". . . the Turkish Foreign Minister assured Hitler's shrewd ambassador Franz von Papen, that every true Turk longed in his heart for a German victory."(9) Meanwhile, on the island of Malta, the garrison prepared itself for siege and a sustained onslaught by the Luftwaffe, unparalleled in its ferocity. Not until the surrender of Italy, two years later, could the British refocus attention on the Dodecanese.

THE AEGEAN 1942-1943

On 23 October 1942, the British Eighth Army commenced its offensive at El Alamein, and on the following day the joint Anglo-American task force sailed for French North Africa to mount the TORCH landings at Algiers, Casablanca, and Oran. On 18 November, the British CIC Middle East ordered its staff to prepare plans for the capture of Crete, Rhodes, and the islands of the Dodecanese. However, upon further examination of the German defensive position on Crete, it became obvious that it would not be possible to mount an assault against this island unless it was selected as a primary objective in the Mediterranean and all resources mobilized toward that end.

The primary objective was to secure Turkey's entry into the War. Coupled with this were a number of secondary targets thought necessary to achieve the main objective. The secondary targets of opportunity were the island of Rhodes and a number of smaller islands which included Kos, Leros, and Samos. These

islands however, were not of equal weight. Rhodes was the
"key." Kos with its airfield was next in importance, and Leros
with its harbor and naval batteries ranked third. The Greek
island of Samos ranked fourth; it was not so strategically
placed as the other islands and, more to the point, it was
sovereign Greek territory.

In assessing the British capacity for an attack on Rhodes,
staff planners in the Middle East Command considered it a
possibility, "even without the use of Turkish airfields provided
that the German Air Force (GAF) was kept fully engaged
elsewhere, otherwise operations in the Aegean were not
feasible."(10) Assuming the employment of the GAF in the
eastern Mediterranean, Turkish airfields would be needed to
provide cover for the British assault force. Middle East
Command could guarantee nothing. Even with major operations
underway in the central Mediterranean, the Germans could very
well reinforce Rhodes and the Dodecanese.

Planning proceeded with estimates of the resources that would
be required for operations in the Aegean. These additional
resources included two auxiliary aircraft carriers, eighty-eight
landing craft of various types, and ten aircraft squadrons.
Churchill minuted General Ismay: "What do the Chiefs of Staff
Committee think about this? I rather like it. I will discuss
it with General Alexander."(11) On 27 January, the Prime
Minister directed the CIC Middle East, General Sir Harold
Alexander, with the task of "planning and preparing for the
capture of the Dodecanese employing 'ingenuity and resource' to
the full."(12)

The Central Planning Staff in Cairo were faced with the
problem of just exactly what plans and preparations should be
made. The degree and scope of operations in the Aegean would
obviously be governed by the demands for the forthcoming
invasion of Sicily. If the invasion was successful there might
be opportunities to seize the Dodecanese or even effect a
landing in Greece. Equally, if HUSKY was not successful, large
scale operations in the eastern Mediterranean would provide a
good diversion, especially with Turkish cooperation. However,
the only Mediterranean operation explicitly approved by the
conference was the invasion of Sicily. On 12 February, General
Sir Henry Maitland Wilson, who had taken over command of Middle
East Forces from General Alexander, received a directive from
the Prime Minister giving his main tasks in order of priority:

- to maintain the Eighth Army and support its
  operations to the utmost limit until Tunisia
  is fully cleared of the enemy.

- in conformity with the requirements of
  General Eisenhower, to take all measures
  necessary for the mounting of that part of

operation HUSKY which is launched from the
area under your command.

● to make preparations for supporting Turkey in
such a manner as may be necessary to give
effect to the policy of His Majesty's Government as communicated to you from time to time
by the Chiefs of Staff.

● to prepare for amphibious operations in the
eastern Mediterranean.(13)

As a result of this directive, on 22 February the CIC Middle
East informed the COS that they intended to prepare detailed
plans for operations in the eastern Mediterranean as a diversion
or as an alternative to HUSKY. On 4 March, the COS gave their
approval, and on 19 March, directives were issued for three
principal Aegean planners, one from each of the three Services:
Lieutenant-General Sir Desmond Anderson; Air Vice Marshal RE
Saul; and Rear Admiral GJA Miles.

There then followed a series of plans and appreciations
prepared by the Joint Planners based on Joint Intelligence
Committee (JIC) analyses as to the preferred course of action
which ought to be followed in the event that: (1) Italy
remained in the War; (2) Germany might abandon Italy; (3)
Germany might hold northern Italy but abandon the south; and (4)
the Germans might respond to an increased threat from the
Balkans.

In all scenarios except the first, the collapse of Italy was a
dependent variable. Projects in the eastern Mediterranean that
might follow an unopposed landing in Italy were again put
forward by the planners. The Chiefs of Staff did not look with
favor on these limited proposals for exploiting the situation in
the Balkans. They dismissed the idea of preparing for the
occupation of the Dodecanese, vetoing at the same time a
proposal from the CIC Middle East, for an attack on Rhodes.
Professor Hinsley observes:

The British COS had three major concerns.
Operations in the Aegean would not be acceptable
to the United States; it would be premature to
encourage Turkey when the Allies were unable to
give her substantial support and third, such
actions might incite the Germans to strengthen
the Romanian Ploesti oilfield defenses and
perhaps to attack in Thrace. But above all they
continued to be skeptical of the JIC's argument
that, if only she had to give priority to
retaining control over the Balkans, Germany would
withdraw to northern Italy.(14)

Meanwhile, Number 2 Planning Staff formed in Cairo, continued
to explore the possibilities for operations in the Aegean.
Planning was complicated by the conflicting ambitions of the
Greeks and Turks for ultimate possession of the Dodecanese.   It
was decided that operations would be conducted by British forces
only and the future of the Dodecanese would not be discussed
with either of the interested parties.

Several plans looked toward the Aegean as an area to be
exploited.   According to Molony: "The Washington conference in
May 1943, had given General Eisenhower first call on all
disposable forces in the Mediterranean Theatre except for seven
Allied divisions earmarked for OVERLORD, and two British
divisions which might be committed to support Turkey against
Axis attack."(15)   These were the Eighth Indian and the Tenth
Indian Divisions.

Adolf Hitler believed that the seven Allied divisions were in
reality, the task force for operations in Turkey and the
Balkans.   Although the prospect of obtaining troops from North
Africa was uncertain, staff planners in the Middle East produced
a detailed plan for a full-scale attack on Rhodes and Scarpanto
(Karpathos) and the subsequent occupation of other islands.
Uncertainty over Turkey's attitude, the complication of the
political situation in the Balkans, and the needs for Sicily and
Italy made detailed planning difficult.   However, on four
occasions a force was assembled and partially prepared to
undertake the capture of Rhodes.

On 26 July, the day after Mussolini was overthrown: "The
Combined Chiefs of Staff ordered Eisenhower to carry the war to
the Italian mainland at the earliest possible date."(16)
General Wilson telegraphed General Sir Alan Brooke: "Reports
from the Balkans, Crete and the Dodecanese during the last few
days show developments which we might be able to turn to our
advantage at short notice if we had the means."(17)

General Wilson indicated that owing to equipment deficiencies
and the absence of assault craft in the Middle East, he was not
in a position to act quickly.   He disclosed the fact that, apart
from the Eighth Indian Division he had no fully equipped
formation in the Middle East and that, for a "quick" ACCOLADE
with full exploitation, he needed in addition, the Tenth Indian
Division, which came under his command, the First Greek Brigade
and the Ninth Armored Brigade equipped to a scale of 80
percent.   The minimum shipping required was: "One HQ Ship;
eight LSI (L) or LSP; eighteen MT Ships; two LSG; eight 'Z'
Craft, a Naval Fuel Tanker; and if available, eighteen LCT's.
Eight LSI (L) are at present in the Middle East including five
earmarked for India."(18)   Churchill minuted his Chief of Staff:

> Here is a business of great consequence to be
> thrust forward by every means, all supplies to
> Turkey may be stopped, this is no time for

conventional establishments, but rather for using whatever fighting elements there are. I hope the Staffs will be able to stimulate action which may gain immense prizes at little costs, though not at little risk.(19)

The British COS directed General Wilson to approach General Eisenhower for the use of any assault craft he could spare from his main operation. In these preliminary moves, the British COS made it clear that operational plans for action in the central Mediterranean should have priority. Wilson responded: "Operation ACCOLADE in its attenuated form will only take place if conditions in the objective give reasonable prospect for success."(20)

The indications were plain. The British intended to go for the Dodecanese. Eisenhower would be invited to provide any assault craft he could spare. Ultimately, plans for ACCOLADE would place the Allied Commander in direct confrontation with the British Prime Minister. These were the straws in the wind, an indication of events which were to bring serious disagreement between the Western Allies in the months ahead.

NOTES

1.   CJC Molony, et al., The Mediterranean and Middle East, vol. 5, History of the Second World War (London: Her Majesty's Stationery Office, 1973), 186.

2.   Ibid., 395.

3.   Henry Maitland Wilson, Bt. Eight Years Overseas 1939-1947 (London: Hutchinson, 1948), 179.

4.   Mark A. Stoler, The Politics of the Second Front (Westport, Connecticut: Greenwood Press, 1977), 176.

5.   Molony, The Mediterranean, 532.

6.   Lord Ismay, The Memoirs of General Lord Ismay (London: William Heinemann, 1960), 322.

7.   Public Record Office, London, DEFE 2/178.

8.   Ibid.

9.   David Irving, Hitler's War (New York: Viking Press, 1977), 339.

10.   Public Record Office, London, AIR 41/53.

11.   Ibid.

12.   Ibid.

13.   Ibid. also Molony, The Mediterranean, 533.

14.   FH Hinsley, British Intelligence in the Second World War, vol. 3, part 1 (Cambridge: Cambridge University Press, 1979), 7.

15.   Molony, The Mediterranean, 532.

16.   Hinsley, British Intelligence, 8.

17.   Public Record Office, London, AIR 41/53.

18.   Ibid.

19.   Ibid.

20.   Ibid.

Plans for Accolade

By the end of July, there were three versions of ACCOLADE: "A walk-in to Rhodes and other islands in the Dodecanese if the Italians collapsed and the Germans withdrew; a quick opportune ACCOLADE in the event that the Italians collapsed but the Germans were standing firm; and a full ACCOLADE against German and Italian opposition. An unlikely prospect."(1)

Meanwhile, Allied air forces were being redeployed for major operations in the central Mediterranean. The Germans had an air base on Scarpanto some 45 miles from Rhodes and airfields in Greece, which were 270 miles from the island. The nearest RAF base was at Gambut in North Africa, 350 miles away, beyond the limits of single-engine fighters. While the P-38s (Lightnings) were more than a match for German Me 109s, only a very few P-38s were available.

Beaufighter performance was poor. It seemed that ACCOLADE in any of its forms was impractical unless the Turks would grant the Allies use of airfields in Anatolia. The British, however, hoped that Allied operations in the central Mediterranean would tie down the Luftwaffe, allowing Eisenhower to release heavy bombers for attacks on German airfields in Greece and Crete and loan to the Aegean four squadrons of P-38s for air cover.

On 1 August, General Wilson identified his immediate needs for assault shipping to load one infantry brigade plus an armored regiment, and declared his intention to prepare the partially equipped Tenth Indian Division, the First Greek Brigade, and the Ninth Armored Brigade for operations in the Aegean. CIC Middle East made it clear that the majority of the air and naval forces, shipping and landing craft would have to come from central Mediterranean, that is, from Allied Force Headquarters (AFHQ), in Algiers.

The British Chiefs of Staff with the Prime Minister's approval sent a cable to Wilson: "CIC Middle East should prepare to the best of their ability to profit from any favorable opportunity in the Aegean."(2) On 2 August, the British COS authorized the

landing ships earmarked for India to be detained in the Middle
East (the so-called "Standstill Order") and Wilson was told to
ask Eisenhower for anything he could spare. On 5 August, Wilson
asked Eisenhower for eight ships, four squadrons of P-38s,
transport aircraft to lift one parachute battalion and special
units, all to arrive in the Middle East by 14-15 August.

Given the ships, Middle East Command would have an assault
brigade ready to sail by 18 August and a follow-up brigade four
days later. Eisenhower agreed to provide the troops and the
ships but not the P-38s or transport aircraft, which were needed
for Salerno and for other operations in the central
Mediterranean. He said: "The Lightning squadrons were fully
employed in escorting the Strategic Bomber Force for the primary
role of knocking Italy out of the war and were specifically
required for AVALANCHE. All transport aircraft available to the
Italian theatre were required for planned operations on that
front."(3)

Within a few days, Eisenhower made it clear that he was no
longer prepared to provide even limited support. In
consultation with his deputies, General Alexander and Air Chief
Marshal Tedder, the implications for supporting operations in
the Aegean were reassessed. On 12 August, Eisenhower informed
the COS and Middle East Command that he viewed with considerable
concern the possibility, that in practice, requirements for
operations in the Aegean will draw upon resources urgently
required for the Italian front. In his opinion, with which his
Deputy CICs agreed: "We should concentrate on one thing at a
time and ACCOLADE should be abandoned for the present."(4)

Meanwhile, the British COS on their way to Quebec received a
warning from the Joint Staff Mission (JSM) in Washington
expressing a concern that the United States Joint Chiefs of
Staff (USJCOS) felt that the British were not standing firm
enough to the considered decisions of TRIDENT, and were tending
too readily to depart from these decisions and to set aside the
operations agreed upon: "They seem particularly to take
exception to the British 'Standstill Order' in the Mediterranean,
to which they refer as a unilateral decision."(5)

The British Chiefs reconsidered the constraining shipping
order, which they had issued before QUADRANT and were now agreed
that it should be revoked. From the JSM signal two things
became clear. First, the Americans were opposed to the British
taking any action without first consulting with them, and
second, any deviation from plans previously approved by the
Joint Chiefs was not to be considered without prior approval of
the Combined Chiefs of Staff.

Revocation of the "Standstill Order" meant that General Wilson
could no longer rely upon the availability of ships previously
held at his disposal for the operation against Rhodes. These
ships were in fact dispersed and ordered to Bombay and the
Indian Ocean. By mid-August it became apparent that the Germans
did not intend to evacuate the Dodecanese but were contemplating

sending reinforcements.   The chance opportunity for jumping
islands was not bright.

On 14 August, the Vice Chiefs of Staff (VCOS) sent a signal to
Wilson saying: "Troop movements for embarkation for ACCOLADE
should be held up pending further decision."(6) Thus, the plans
that the Middle East Commanders had prepared for operations in
the Aegean were now no longer viable. General Wilson considered
the implications with regard to shipping and German intentions,
but continued to proceed with his plans. On 23 August, the CIC
MEHQ informed the British Chiefs of Staff and Allied Commanders
that he was carrying out rehearsals on 25 and 26 August.
According to Wilson: "The possibility of mounting an operation
is dependent upon the presence of the Eighth Indian Division in
the Middle East."(7)

The British Chiefs wished to be appraised as to what
operations might then be feasible. Wilson's stipulation with
respect to the Eighth Indian Division was noted. However, on 26
August, Eisenhower warned Wilson that he would soon require this
division. August was drawing to a close. On the 31st, Wilson
signaled to COS and the Allied Commanders: "Release of ships to
India renders any assault operations based on Middle East
impossible."(8)

On 3 September, the Allies invaded Italy, and on 8 September,
Italy surrendered. Anticipating this collapse, an inter-service
liaison team under Major Jellicoe was sent to Rhodes to see if
General Scaroina and Admiral Campioni could be encouraged to
"round up" the German garrison, which comprised an assault
division of 7,000 troops. If the team reported favorably,
234 Infantry Brigade and some tanks would sail for Rhodes in
three available merchant ships, the success of which "would
depend upon being able to use Rhodes harbor without opposition,
and likewise one airfield upon which one or two Spitfire
squadrons would be ready to land."(9) The Italian garrison
numbered 30,000 troops.

This moment was critical. If the three-man team reported
favorably with respect to Italian intentions and capabilities,
which must include a firm resolve to fight with the Allies, the
despatch of a British brigade group to Rhodes would surely
follow. The following day, the German Commander, General
Klemann, ordered his men to attack the Italian Regina Division.
This they did, seizing General Scaroina in the process. As a
consequence, on 11 September, Admiral Campioni capitulated and
surrendered his entire garrison to the Germans. Later, General
Wilson in his despatches, said of the Italian Governor: "His
spirit was clearly affected by the delay and by the fact
that the Germans were there whilst we were not."(10)

Throughout, the efficacy of British plans for operations in
the Aegean rested upon the active involvement of Italian troops
in support of the Allies. However, a large majority of Italians
were apathetic and did not want to fight on either side. It
would have been dangerous to employ such doubtful allies in

important positions in the front line. General Wilson informed the Prime Minister that the Commander of Force 292 was of the opinion that the Italian offensive potential was nil and their equipment generally poor. At the same time, the CIC Middle East considered that the presence of Greek troops in the Dodecanese would materially increase the difficulty of relations with Italian garrisons whose cooperation in defense of the islands was considered essential.

The British seemed not to heed this advice; they had relied heavily upon active Italian cooperation in the islands. A signal was sent to AFHQ, Algiers, asking whether, "a firm statement could be made by Marshal Badoglio or the King to the Italian commanders ordering their troops to fight to the last man in defense of these islands."(11)

There is no point in castigating Admiral Campioni. Seven thousand German troops would have made short work of any heroics on his part or on the part of his men who, far from fighting to the last man, would be disinclined to fight at all. Moreover, if 234 Brigade had landed on Rhodes, it is extremely doubtful that the British infantry would have been able to engage successfully, far less "round up," a German assault division that was triple their strength in numbers and well rehearsed in tactical maneuver.

Manifestly, the British continued to be guided by the most appalling appreciations as to Italian capabilities and, indeed, as to their own. Even with the despatch of the remaining brigades from Tenth Indian Division, the British force would have been inadequate to the task, inferior in numbers, and lacking in close air support. Churchill, always behind the scenes, came onto the stage determined to make a drama out of a crisis: "This is the time to play high. Improvise and dare."(12) Wilson cabled his intentions and dispositions to General Eisenhower and the Chief of the Imperial General Staff, General Sir Alan Brooke:

> We have improvised one brigade group lightly equipped at the expense of the 10th Indian Division. Any opposed landing is of course quite out of the question but we think there is an outside chance of the Italians in Rhodes resisting the Germans.(13)

On 12 September, General Wilson informed the COS that he considered no further action could be taken against Rhodes. Action would, however, be taken in the other islands. Meanwhile, the Prime Minister refused to take note of Wilson's appreciation concerning Rhodes, or of the unreliable Italians who had virtually been written off. On 13 September, Churchill cabled General Wilson: "The capture of Rhodes by you at this time with Italian aid would be a fine contribution to the general war. Let me know what are your plans for this."(14)

Royal Air Force (RAF) Middle East signaled the Air Ministry:
"Without Allied military and air reinforcement, Italian
resistance to the Germans will be negligible. Moreover, the
Germans are taking energetic action to obtain possession of all
the important Aegean islands."(15) The signal drew specific
attention to the fact that, with the exception of Rhodes, by
then in German hands, Kos was the only island in the Dodecanese
having a suitable airfield. More troops, including a company of
paratroops, were to be sent to Kos and considerable importance
was attached by the British to Leros.

The German reaction on Rhodes and the inability of the British
to restore the situation made it necessary for General Wilson to
revise completely his plans for the Aegean. Future plans, of
necessity, would have to be on a smaller scale, and they would
have to be improvised. Wilson then proceeded to despatch the
main elements of 234 Infantry Brigade to the smaller islands to
join the Special Boat Service (SBS), Long Range Desert Group
(LRDG) and B Company Second Battalion of the Royal West Kent (2
RWK) who were already there: Second Battalion of the Royal
Irish Fusiliers(2 RIF) to Leros; First Battalion of the Durham
Light Infantry (1 DLI) to Kos; and 2 RWK, (minus B Company), to
Samos. As 234 Brigade was taking up positions in the islands,
the British Foreign Secretary, Sir Anthony Eden, telegraphed to
the Minister of State in Cairo, repeating the signal to
Washington:

> I should like to see certain general principles
> established both for Dodecanese islands and for
> any Greek or Yugoslav territory which may be
> liberated. British military administrations
> should be set up in the Dodecanese and in the
> liberated Greek islands. Since we shall have to
> make use of Italian garrisons in these islands,
> we must be able to convince the Greek Government
> of our good faith and must avoid giving the
> impression that their interests are being
> sacrificed in favor of the Italians.(16)

This expression of good faith contained a fine point. Eden
felt that the status of the Dodecanese was different from that
of the Greek islands and that this distinction should be
maintained. Greek claims to participate in the occupation and
administration of the Dodecanese was considered to be weaker
than in the case of liberated Greek territory. Eden conceded:
"Some gesture should be made, since they will be more suspicious
of our intentions as regards the Dodecanese than in the case of
the Greek islands."(17) The reader will recall that the
Dodecanese had been administered by the Italians since 1912.

Obviously, Eden was mindful of the British plans to bring
Turkey into the War which he had discussed in Cabinet only
four months earlier, plans that undoubtedly must take into

account Turkey's claim to sovereignty over the Dodecanese. The "post-Ottoman" Italian interlude in the islands, shortly to be terminated, was not to be construed as a possible scenario for giving equal opportunity to the Greeks in re-establishing their cultural heritage in the Dodecanese. Eden was also concerned with proposals to arm guerrillas on the Greek island of Samos. The disadvantages of giving support to the various guerrilla factions on the Greek mainland were already apparent. The ineffectual King George II might never return from exile if diffuse Communist elements among the guerrilla forces were to gain strength.

What were the Americans thinking as events unfolded? "General Marshall watched warily the Prime Minister's attempts to promote landings in the eastern Mediterranean."(18) Churchill could argue that the CCS had initially given their blessing for the British to capture Rhodes. He was less inclined to respect the proviso that, "the effort should be made with the resources available to the Middle East Commander (General Maitland Wilson)."(19) It will be recalled that, on 26 August, the Eighth Indian Division was assigned to the central Mediterranean, while 234 Brigade, being part of the Tenth Indian Division, was committed to the Dodecanese in September. Wilson's slender resources were eroding before his eyes.

Apparently Wilson had to rely upon the release of troops from the central Mediterranean, adding yet another logistics straw to Eisenhower's camel. However, Wilson now faced a major setback. On 3 October, the Durham Light Infantry on Kos was attacked by a German battle group and capitulated within twenty-four hours. The Germans were fully in command on Rhodes, the Eighth Indian Division had been ordered to the central Mediterranean and the landing craft necessary for an assault on Rhodes had been dispersed to the Indian Ocean. British plans to establish a foothold in the Aegean had been dislodged within less than a month.

Many British commanders, including Brooke, Portal, and Tedder wanted to cut the losses in the Aegean. The fall of Kos produced exactly the opposite reaction from the British Prime Minister. The remaining islands of Leros and Samos were to be held at all costs. Moreover, the capture of Rhodes was still to be attempted.

Just prior to the fall of Kos, General Wilson had been authorized by the British Chiefs of Staff in consultation with General Eisenhower to capture Rhodes before the end of October. One way or another, Churchill was determined to bring the Americans to the aid of the party. Clearly, the British by themselves did not have the necessary resources to mount an assault operation against the island.

General Wilson informed the British Chiefs and General Eisenhower that the enemy had complete control of sea as well as air in the Aegean. The loss of the airfields on Kos and the effect of the enemy's reinforcements on Rhodes made any planned assault on that island precarious. There was an urgent need for bombers and long range fighters. General Alan Brooke's diary records:

> 4 October: Found PM in great flutter owing to attack on Kos Island and the effect of its loss on the proposed operations to capture Rhodes.
>
> 6 October: It is quite clear in my mind that with the commitments we have in Italy we should not undertake serious operations in the Aegean. PM by now determined to go to Rhodes without looking at the effects on Italy. I had a heated argument with him.(20)

Attention turned to the provision of aircraft carriers to support the "October ACCOLADE", but there was a problem. The CIC Levant was informed that escort aircraft carriers were on passage to United Kingdom to re-equip with aircraft, to fit very high frequency (VHF) equipment, and to prepare for service in the Indian Ocean. It was not desirable to use a fleet carrier for the Aegean operation. In the face of considerable shore-based air opposition, the ship would have been hard put to look after itself and in no position, with inferior fighters, to assist materially in the assault on Rhodes. It was considered that air cover for operations in the Aegean must depend upon what could be promised from onshore airfields.

Turkey had proved unwilling to provide the British with access to its airfields in September would it be willing to do so in October? Clearly a critical question. On 4 October (the day after Kos had fallen), General Wilson signaled to the British Chiefs of Staff and to General Eisenhower his "Outline Plan for the Capture of Rhodes."

The plan, with D Day on 20 October, was predicated on the enemy strength being not greater than 8,000. The essential elements of the plan were as follows: to land at Lardo Bay, to capture Calato airfield, to advance to destroy German forces, and to occupy the town of Rhodes. The operation was to be carried out by troops of Tenth Indian Division, a Regiment of Ninth Armored Brigade, Eleventh Parachute Battalion, and "other attached units" equipped to minimum scale. The 234 Brigade, which belonged to this division, was already dispersed among the islands. Thus, the remaining divisional strength would produce no more than 60 percent of its effectiveness unless reinforcements could be dredged up from the base camps in the Levant.

The first convoy was to carry four infantry battalions, one squadron of tanks, one field battery, one anti-tank battery, one battery Royal Horse Artillery (RHA), one field company with one Light Anti-Aircraft (LAA) battery and one Heavy Anti-Aircraft (HAA) troop for airfield defense. A parachute battalion to be dropped at Malena area would complete the first phase assault.

The second convoy, to arrive shortly after D Day would have to be carried by the same ships used in the first convoy. It was to carry four infantry battalions, one squadron of tanks, a field regiment of artillery less one battery, and one field company of engineers. The SBS and LRDG were to be infiltrated into Rhodes before D Day to mark beaches and Dropping Zones (DZs) for paratroops, to cause diversions, and to dislocate enemy movements in the northern part of the island.

Reserve troops in Levant were: one field regiment Royal Artillery (RA), one medium battery RA, Ninth Armored Brigade less one regiment, and the Greek Brigade Group. General Wilson had not been able to formulate a "Naval Plan," but Force 292 had identified the need for an aircraft carrier, fleet destroyers, and landing ships for the infantry (LSIs).

The "Air Plan" was to neutralize the GAF in Greece and "elsewhere" by sustained bombardments of airfields by American heavy and medium bombers operating from Italy, two squadrons of British heavy night bombers, and two American Liberator Groups operating from Benghazi. Transport for one battalion of parachute troops was to be supplied by the Americans, while convoy protection was to be afforded by RAF Beaufighters operating from Cyprus. Fighter cover for landing and assault shipping by six squadrons of P-38s based on Cyprus was deemed essential to success.

After the capture of Calato airfield, two squadrons of Spitfires and half a squadron of night-fighters (Beaufighters) were then to be moved to Calato from Cyprus. In addition to the above, carrier-borne aircraft were considered essential for providing air cover for convoys and for containing enemy reconnaissance. The outline plan was reviewed, first with respect to the provision of aircraft carriers. Vice Admiral Sir Neville Syfret, Vice Chief Naval Staff (VCNS), said:

> This was undesirable in that it would necessitate additional destroyers for escort duties and furthermore, after they had provided fighters for their own protection they would have few aircraft available to support landing operations. If in spite of the objections, it was decided to employ carriers in the eastern Mediterranean, HMS Formidable could be made available. Alternatively, three escort carriers which had been lent for AVALANCHE, now on their way home, could be returned in time for ACCOLADE.(21)

The COS then telegraphed to the CIC Middle East asking whether aircraft carriers were considered essential to their plan, and what would be the effect if no carriers were provided? The COS further noted that the plan would entail considerable assistance from General Eisenhower. On 5 October, Eisenhower responded to the COS with a copy to the Combined Chiefs of Staff, saying he was very concerned over an aggressive policy in the Aegean. He felt that he would be asked to undertake a considerable and continuing air and sea commitment which he may not be able to afford. He drew attention to the problem facing him on the mainland of Italy.

The latest information demonstrated the German's decision to engage in major battle for Italy in support of their armies in the field. Eisenhower needed to employ the entire available Allied air effort on the Italian front. With only eleven Allied divisions to the German's twenty-two, the Allied strength was clearly inversely proportional to its needs.

General Eisenhower was prepared to support ACCOLADE. However, he again pointed out that the effect of diversions of Allied air strength from the Italian theatre would be serious: "If ACCOLADE is undertaken, that operation however desirable in itself is bound to place calls on us for a very considerable and continuing diversion of air effort, I consider any material diversion highly prejudicial to the success of Italian operations."(22) The British Prime Minister was quite unwilling to accept Eisenhower's concern and took every conceivable step to influence events. On 6 October, Churchill minuted his Chiefs of Staff through General Ismay:

> All this plan for taking Rhodes is affected by loss of Kos. The Chiefs of Staff should consider whether the forces available are sufficient to overcome 8,000 plus Germans even when safely landed. It is for serious consideration whether forces now gathered for Rhodes, though not enough for Rhodes, may be enough for Kos. There are 2-3,000 German troops who have landed whose capture would retrieve the loss of the island and avenge our Durham Light Infantry.(23)

The British force was to land in two stages, four days apart. Without doubt, 8,000 Germans would have made short work of four infantry battalions, estimated at 2,400 men, plus a parachute battalion. The odds would have been greatly against the British. The follow-up convoy of four infantry battalions four days later would have fared no better. Churchill was well aware that the British force to take Rhodes would be too light on the ground. And, as noted, 234 Brigade was already involved: the DLI hors de combat on Kos, while 2 RIF and 2 RWK were in position on Leros and Samos.

The Prime Minister's secondary intention, to use the ACCOLADE assault force against Kos rather than Rhodes, shows a total lack of understanding from the tactical point of view. To retake Kos without having first secured Rhodes would have left the British more vulnerable than ever before. Even with the recapture of Kos there would still be the problem of holding it. Churchill was impatient. To him, Kos was a trophy. The Germans had snatched it away from the DLI, and he wanted it back again. In the entire Aegean venture he was willing to play around with bits and pieces. While paying lip service to the fact that Rhodes was the key, the British Prime Minister was nevertheless prepared to inflate the value of the smaller islands in order to maintain a foothold in the Dodecanese.

The British COS met yet again to consider the situation. Sir Alan Brooke, Sir Charles Portal and Sir Neville Syfret examined the Rhodes/Kos options, the impact of either on the Italian front and provision of landing craft, air cover and aircraft carriers. Meanwhile, Churchill sent a signal to General Eisenhower, copied to CIC Middle East and JSM, Washington:

> Most immediate--Clear the Line: We think it essential that General Eisenhower should forthwith convene a conference, at whatever place he may think most desirable, between himself and his CIC on the one hand and CIC in the Middle East on the other hand to formulate proposals for action in eastern Mediterranean.(24)

The United States Joint Chiefs of Staff responded by saying that they, "could not [direct] General Eisenhower to provide for the Middle East Command any forces or military equipment which in his opinion were needed for the Italian campaign."(25) The USJCOS, however, raised no objection to General Eisenhower providing any available assistance. The next day the Prime MInister signaled to General Eisenhower, drawing a fine picture of the Balkans "bogeyman":

> The Germans have to apprehend desertion by Hungary and Romania and a violent schism in Bulgaria. At any moment Turkey may lean her weight against them. I have never wished to send an army into the Balkans, but only by agents, supplies and commandos, to stimulate the intense guerrilla action prevailing there. . . . Rhodes is the key to all this. I do not feel the present plan of taking it is good enough. It will require and is worth a least up to a first class division . . . your diversion would only be temporary, I am telegraphing to the President.(26)

General Wilson signaled to the CIGS, General Sir Alan Brooke, that in company with his Service Chiefs (Admiral Sir John Cunningham and AVM Linnell), he would proceed to Tunis on the night of 8-9 October for a conference with General Eisenhower. Meanwhile, the COS had received a report by the Joint Planning Staff on Wilson's "Outline Plan" and two minutes from the VCNS to the Prime Minister. The committee was aware that HMS FORMIDABLE had returned to Gibraltar and that the PM had directed that it remain there pending the results of the conference. They agreed that no instructions regarding movement of landing craft could be issued until after the conference.

At the next meeting with his Chiefs of Staff, Churchill reiterated the points he had made in his signal to President Roosevelt emphasizing that the capture of Rhodes should be done by first class troops: "If possible by utilizing a division now destined for Italy."(27) He could not believe that the diversion of one division, together with the necessary assault craft, for a period of some two months would have a vital effect on the Italian operations. He neglected to make any mention of the order of battle for operation HARDIHOOD or the impact which further reinforcement of operations in the eastern Mediterranean would have on the Italian campaign, or on the planning for OVERLORD.

Churchill always expressed "l'idee fixe"; and having bought the first premise one was then expected to accept the legitimacy of all further reasoning. Alan Brooke felt that the diversion of a first class division from Italy would leave the Allies open to the danger of being successfully counterattacked at the Pisa line, and of being thrown back, possibly even as far as Rome. He suggested that, rather than attacking Rhodes, the Allies should support the guerrilla forces in Albania and Yugoslavia with a view to forcing the enemy to withdraw from southern Greece.

Sir Andrew Cunningham, the First Sea Lord, while in support of the Aegean option, "did not see where the necessary forces were to come from, and would like to investigate the shipping position further."(28) Summing up, the Prime Minister said that: "A cardinal strategic decision was now at issue. It was intolerable that the enemy pressed on all fronts, would be allowed to pick up cheap prizes in the Aegean. Rhodes was the key and every effort should be made to capture it."(29)

Churchill failed to recognize that Rhodes was never a cheap prize. It was garrisoned by a German assault division. If Rhodes was of cardinal strategic value, it was up to the Allies to recognize it as such and prepare adequate plans. If, in the Prime Minister's opinion, it deserved a "first class division" to capture it in October, the same can be said for September. As we have seen, it was Churchill who tried to take Rhodes cheaply: first, to "walk-in," which was never feasible under any circumstances; and second, by mounting an assault with the remnants of the Tenth Indian Division.

The British had, indeed, picked up cheap prizes in the form of Kos, Leros, and Samos, where initially their occupation was unopposed. But from this point on they were unable to hold the islands. British naval losses, the sacrifice of the 234 Brigade, and indeed, German losses also, are all testimony to the fact that everyone paid a high price to hold these peripheral islands. Without Rhodes, possession of the smaller islands was never really significant; with Rhodes they were commensurately

of much greater value. Nevertheless, the Germans felt
threatened and moved quickly to obliterate the British presence.

What is difficult to understand is how the British Prime
Minister could, by some convoluted reasoning, delude himself
into thinking that, with a lodgment on the smaller islands, his
troops could somehow bring about the fall of Rhodes. His
reasoning was equally faulty if he felt that the Germans would
allow General Wilson to build-up positions on Kos and Leros
against a moment in time when it might be more opportune to
mount an assault force to capture Rhodes itself.

If the British incursion into the Aegean in September 1943 had
been in concert with the entry of Turkey into the War or with
the Turks showing a willingness to bend their neutrality
allowing the Allies use of Turkish airfields, the risk factor
might have been better justified. But Turkey was not inclined
to enter the War, nor was she willing to be pushed into
precipitate action by playing a hand that Winston Churchill had
seriously overbid. The tacit agreement for assistance reached
with the Turks at Adana was nothing more than that: On 9
October, President Roosevelt signaled to the Prime Minister:

> With full understanding of your difficulties in
> the eastern Mediterranean, my thoughts . . . [are
> that there should be] no diversion of force from
> Italy which would jeopardize the security of
> Allied armies in Italy. No action toward any
> minor objective should prejudice the success of
> OVERLORD.(30)

The President was at pains to point out that the difficulties
in the Aegean were of Churchill's own making and that they had
not arisen in consequence of an agreed Allied plan. He also
drew specific attention to the diversion of force not only with
respect to OVERLORD, against which Churchill had sought to
justify the reassignment of landing craft, but also to Italy,
which was a major theatre of operations. Finally, he focused on
the scale of operations in the Aegean: "As I see it, it is not
merely the capture of Rhodes, but it must mean of necessity, and
it must be apparent to the Germans, that we intend to go
further. Otherwise Rhodes will be under the guns of both Kos
and Crete."(31)

British Intelligence estimated that the German Air Force
front-line strength in the Greece-Aegean area was in the order
of 350 aircraft. Churchill disputed this. However, he went on
to say: "I hold myself perfectly free to give up the Rhodes
stroke if the conditions are too bad when the time comes."(32)
Nevertheless, the Prime Minister always hoped that he would be
able to lay his hands on air squadrons operating from the
central Mediterranean and thus put off the critical moment when
it would have been better to abandon operations in the Aegean.
By 10 October, Churchill appeared to face up to the situation on

the Italian front: "We must bow to the new fact of the German intention to reinforce his divisions and fight the battle south of Rome."(33)

The Prime Minister wanted to know if Kos could be recaptured. He recognized that there was little point in asking the Turks for use of airfields saying: "Unless Wilson can make a good plan, we cannot go on indefinitely with the special naval operations. If nothing could be done, the Leros garrison should be evacuated."(34) In particular, he was concerned that the LRDG should be extricated from the islands rather than fall prisoner to the Germans.

This was the Prime Minister's stated position one month before Leros was attacked. Nothing in the ensuing four week period served to alleviate the fundamental weakness of the British position--namely the absence of a force to capture Rhodes. Rather, the period was used to reinforce Leros at the cost of frightful losses to the Royal Navy. This precarious lodgment in the Aegean without either Kos or Rhodes, served as a most pathetic stratagem: since the British had demonstrated their intent to hold Samos and Leros, wouldn't both the Turks and the Americans quickly step in? If, on the other hand, Leros was evacuated, the venture would simply fall away.

Wilson hoped, with the continued goodwill of the Turks, to maintain the garrisons. He would not contemplate evacuation of his Aegean force unless it became apparent that through the deflection of the Italians or because of a change of heart by the Turks or through enemy action that defense of the islands was no longer possible. Wilson's insight into the reality of the situation appears to have been clouded by muddle and myopia. The Italians on both Rhodes and Kos had already been deflected, and throughout the Dodecanese and the Peloponnese, a significant number of Italian officers were being summarily executed by the Germans.

The Allied CIC held a meeting at AFHQ La Marsa, in Algiers, on 10 October, one week after the fall of Kos. The meeting, attended by the CIC of the Mediterranean, Middle East, and Levant Commands, was to explore and restore the situation in the Aegean by mounting an assault that would result in the capture of Rhodes. All resources were reviewed, and the effects of diversions on the Italian campaign by this action were considered, together with a pause in Italy while Rhodes was secured.

One foreseeable problem was strong German reaction, including GAF reinforcements from Russia and France, giving the enemy complete control of the air and, consequently, of the sea in the Aegean. The poor fighting quality of the Italians and the inadequacy of their fixed defenses, together with the remoteness of Allied air bases and a deterioration in the weather, were also noted.

These factors compounded to affect the ability of the British to remedy the situation. The Allied Chiefs were agreed: "If

Rhodes is not captured and held, there is no chance of restoring the local air situation sufficiently to allow surface forces and maintenance shipping to defend and maintain the islands we still hold."(35) In assessing the scale of operations necessary for the capture of Rhodes, the Allied Commanders observed:

> The first essential was to obtain mastery of the
> air. For this, it would be necessary to employ
> the bulk of Mediterranean bomber forces to attack
> airfields in Athens, Salonika, Crete and Rhodes,
> as well as employing all P-38 squadrons in the
> Mediterranean. (The Commanders went further.)
> Even with the addition of carrier-borne aircraft
> which might be available, we consider this cover
> quite inadequate.(36)

The Commanders observed: "The present assault plan to take Rhodes, which is based on limited Middle East resources is too weak to give reasonable chance a success."(37) A minimum force of one infantry division with elements of armor was thought to be necessary and for this, much greater resources in landing ships and craft would have been required.

The conference then moved to a detailed examination of the effects of undertaking Aegean operations on the campaign in Italy. The Allied Commanders noted that while ground forces could be provided from formations which could not at that moment be placed in Italy, the provision of landing craft, if taken from the pool left in the Mediterranean, "would react most seriously upon the continued build-up and maintenance of Italy. Moreover, it would preclude amphibious operations that are an integral part of Alexander's plan."(38) This was in reference to the Anzio landings, which took place on 22 January 1944.

The diversion of Allied air resources to the Aegean would have drastically reduced the Allies' ability to mount operations against German communications and the build-up of enemy concentrations in Italy. In short, air superiority was a critical factor in retaining the initiative and the offensive on the Italian front. At the La Marsa Conference, it was agreed that Allied resources in the Mediterranean were not large enough to allow the capture of Rhodes and at the same time secure Allied objectives in Italy. The Commanders agreed: "We must concentrate on the Italian campaign. We therefore recommend that ACCOLADE be postponed."(39) Without Rhodes and Kos it was obviously impossible to defend and maintain Leros and Samos, but no one wanted to stress the obvious and thus incur the wrath of the Prime Minister.

Two days after the La Marsa Conference, the British Foreign Secretary, Sir Anthony Eden, met in Cairo with the First Sea Lord, Admiral of the Fleet, Sir Andrew Cunningham, the CIC Middle East, General Sir Henry Maitland Wilson, Air Vice Marshal Linnell, and the COC of CIC Levant, Vice Admiral Algernon

Willis. It was agreed that there would be no chance of success in any attempt to recapture Kos unless Turkey agreed to the use of her airfields. They also agreed that, it would be unwise to approach Turkey for permission, since the Turks would almost certainly demand fulfillment of the Adana conclusions in their anxiety for the safety of Istanbul.

Most significantly, the Chiefs noted: "Even if we had the use of Turkish airfields there were not sufficient air forces available in the Middle East to support the capture of Kos."(40) Eden and the Middle East CIC then estimated the demands that would have to be placed on General Eisenhower if air forces from the central Mediterranean theatre were called upon. Again it was noted that these resources could not be diverted from the central Mediterranean without prejudicing Allied operations in Italy. Moreover, assuming Turkish support, six weeks would elapse before the British could establish airfields in Anatolia. Thus, an operation to retake Kos could not commence before the beginning of December. Eden said: "This is running close to the big thing."(41) It seems reasonably clear that his remark was in reference to Anzio.

Finally, the Chiefs took specific note of the fact that the necessary landing craft for an operation against Kos could be made available only at the expense of OVERLORD and BULLFROG. Eden's conclusion was: "To keep our eyes fixed on Rhodes and let Kos go for the present."(42) Yet only two days earlier, at the AFHQ Conference at La Marsa, it had been agreed that, in light of fundamental objectives in the central Mediterranean, plans for operations in the Aegean be set aside. Eisenhower said: "We must concentrate on the Italian campaign. ACCOLADE (or HANDCUFF) must be postponed."(43)

Part Three of the Eden agenda dealt with Leros. The Chiefs noted that an enemy attack on the island seemed imminent. Linnell had asked Tedder to consider the possibility of an immediate attack on German landing craft assembled at Kalymnos, saying: "There can be no question of evacuation from Leros so long as this attack is imminent."(44) Eden telegraphed to the Prime Minister: "If the German attack either fails to materialize or is beaten off, we are in no doubt that we should hold onto Leros."(45)

Turning to the question of ground troops, the CIC proposed to reinforce Leros with specialist personnel for manning existing artillery and by the provision of AA, anti-tank, and twenty-five pounder guns. At this point, British forces on Leros comprised, the Second Battalion Royal Irish Fusiliers, B Company, the Second Battalion Royal West Kent Regiment, and a squadron of the Long Range Desert Group--less than 700 fighting troops in all. (The balance of the Royal West Kents who were originally destined for Kos in September were diverted to Samos.)

Following the fall of Kos, Churchill cabled Wilson: "For your eyes alone and Secretary of State for Foreign Affairs to see only if still in Cairo. My thoughts dwell constantly on Leros and generally on this foothold in the Aegean. It would be a great triumph if you could keep this safely. Although I yielded with good grace to the recent decision, I am still not sure."(46) Eden, architect of the earlier British catastrophe in Greece, had no competence to judge a tactical situation, while Wilson was always obedient to Churchill. In the British High Command, only Eden and Wilson fully supported the Prime Minister's costly foray into the Aegean.

What conclusions can be drawn from the recommendations made at the La Marsa Conference on 10 October and the Cairo Conference with Eden on 12 October? First, it had already been made clear at La Marsa that the Allies could either fight in Italy or in the Aegean, but not in both areas at the same time. The Aegean must be construed to mean not only Rhodes but the other islands as well. The Allied Chiefs did not equivocate in their appreciation that if Rhodes was not captured and held, there was no possibility of holding onto Leros. Everyone agreed that an Aegean operation would take all the P-38s in the Mediterranean and, even with the availability of carrier-borne aircraft, the cover would be quite inadequate.

At the Cairo Conference, Eden's group had evaluated and dismissed the prospect for an assault to retake Kos, yet it considered it necessary to hold onto Leros. With this endeavor, Churchill fully agreed. The political judgment of the Prime Minister and the British Foreign Secretary was still very much at variance with the prevailing military assessment of the situation. At the 254th meeting of the British Chiefs of Staff, Sir Charles Portal said: "The ability of the Leros garrison to withstand an attack if it came, was wholly dependent upon air support. If this could not be made available, it was very doubtful if we were justified in trying to hold the island."(47)

General Sir Alan Brooke was doubtful if Leros was of sufficient importance to justify the naval losses then being incurred. ACM Sir Arthur Tedder was both direct and realistic concerning the state of affairs in the Aegean. Twelve days before Leros was assaulted, he signaled the Chief of Air Staff, first identifying the three main objects of Allied strategy in the Mediterranean: (1) To assist the Army in Italy; (2) To assist POINTBLANK; and (3) To weaken the German hold on the Balkans and the Aegean. In identifying the order of priority, Tedder recognized that the allocation of effort between these objectives depended also on the relative urgency, the weather, the location of air bases, and the movement and supply to forward bases. He was aware that urgencies vary and are apt to be deceptive. He said: "The Aegean extreme urgency has now dragged on for weeks."(48)

In regard to the problem of getting strategic forces forward, Tedder focused on shipping and airfields. He recognized that shipping was subject to a continual fight for priorities. He emphasized that medium bombers and long-range fighters were, indeed, positioned to help the Aegean. Other groups of B-26s (Marauders) and P-38s (Lightnings) had been moved into Sardinia to cover operations over northern Italy and to provide escorts into southern Germany.

In respect to the specific problem of the Aegean, this whole question was fully examined and the limited scale of air effort explained and agreed upon by the Allied Commanders. During October, 1,500 sorties were flown by the USAAF and the RAF, against enemy targets in the Balkans, primarily against enemy aircraft on the ground. The interpretation of PR indicated that over one hundred aircraft had been destroyed on the ground with a probability that actual numbers destroyed were well above this figure.

Despite all this support, Tedder complained that the Allies were continually being subjected to pressure to revise the decisions of the La Marsa meeting to divert further air forces to the Middle East. Tedder perceived that the Kos/Leros operation was a gamble for very big political stakes. He could not say how far failure to hold was or was not due to weaknesses in planning or execution. But to him it was clear that, once Kos had fallen and effective air cover was not longer possible, one of the main foundations of all Aegean operations had collapsed.

After the gamble had failed, Churchill pressed the Allies to throw good money after bad. Douglas wanted to send the B-24 groups back to Cyrenaica and also to send the P-38 groups now in Sardinia. Tedder was convinced that even the addition of these forces could not materially affect a situation, which he said, "was fundamentally unsound owing mainly to the simple, but quite unalterable, fact of geography, in attempting to maintain a garrison and operate surface ships outside the effective range of Allied fighter forces and under the very noses of enemy shore based aircraft."(49)

Alan Brooke echoed Tedder's concern: "Unless we could obtain the early use of Turkish airfields, we should only be throwing good money after bad if we continued to try and hold Leros and Samos."(50) Awaiting events with respect to German intentions to fight for Rome, and going along with Allied decisions to concentrate on the "main operation" (the Italian campaign), Churchill continued to exert pressure with the avowed intention of maintaining a foothold in the Aegean, no doubt influenced by his strategy to induce Turkey to enter the War.

By 2 October, the British had a total of 3,773 ranks dispersed among nine islands. Of this total, 1,511 (40 percent) were on Kos, 1,011 (27 percent) on Leros, 511 (14 percent) on Samos, 389 (10 percent) on Kastellorizo, and 220 (6 percent) on Kalymnos, with the balance on the other islands. By 5 November, the total number of British troops committed to the Dodecanese had increased to a little over 5,000. The relative disposition of the troops was then: Leros, 2,500 (50 percent), Kos, 1,511 (30 percent; now POW), Samos, 500 (10 percent) and Kastellorizo,

300 (6 percent). Small numbers of LRDG and SBS continued to maintain wireless telegraphy stations on the smaller islands.

Churchill can be faulted for his "grand design" which deviated from approved Allied strategy and his persistence with a flawed plan. First, he refused to be guided by the Allied Chiefs, who repeatedly expressed the opinion that an Aegean venture could not be mounted in conjunction with Allied operations in Italy. Second, he encouraged piecemeal initiatives to gain a foothold in the Aegean. Third, he continued to use a tenuous hold on Leros as the key to mounting an assault on Rhodes, hoping thereby to bring Turkey into the War.

The Prime Minister signaled to Wilson: "I am very pleased with the way in which you used such poor bits and pieces as were left to you. Nil desperandum"(51) The Turks were not impressed. "Desperandum" was soon to be the common lot of the Royal Navy and the Leros task force who, in the following four-week period, were to fight for Leros, to die for it, and to lose it.

NOTES

1.   CJC Molony et al., The Mediterranean and Middle East, vol. 5, History of the Second World War (London: Her Majesty's Stationery Office, 1973), 533-544.

2.   Ibid., 536.

3.   Public Record Office, London, PREM 3/3/3, Dwight D. Eisenhower.

4.   Ibid.

5.   Molony, The Mediterranean, 536.

6.   PREM 3/3/3, Vice Chiefs of Staff, (23 August 1943), 6.

7.   Ibid., Henry Maitland Wilson, 8.

8.   Ibid., Wilson, 9.

9.   Ibid., Wilson, 10.

10.   Henry Maitland Wilson, Bt., Despatches Supplement to London Gazette, (London: His Majesty's Stationery Office, 13 November 1946), 2.

11.   Public Record Office, London, PREM 3/3/3; and WO 106/3151.

12.   Ibid., Churchill (9 September 1943).

13.   Ibid., Wilson.

14.   Molony, The Mediterranean, 538.

15.   PREM 3/3/3; and WO 106/3151 (14 September 1943).

16.   Public Record Office, London, CAB 120/500 Eden (25 September 1943).

17.   WO/106/3151.

18.   Forrest C. Pogue, George C. Marshall: Organizer of Victory, 1943-1945 (New York: Viking Press, 1973), 294.

19.   Ibid.

20.   Sir Arthur Bryant, Triumph in the West (London: Doubleday, 1959), 31.

21.   WO 106/3151, Admiral Sir Neville Syfret.

22.   Ibid., Eisenhower.

23.   Ibid., Churchill.

24.   Ibid., Churchill.

25.   Ibid., USJCOS to War Cabinet, London (6 October 1943).

26.   Ibid., Churchill.

27.   Ibid., Churchill.

28.   Ibid., Churchill (7 October 1943).

29.   Ibid., Churchill.

30.   PREM 3/3/5, Roosevelt.

31.   Ibid.

32.   WO/106/3153, Churchill.

33.   CAB 120/501, Churchill.

34.   Ibid., Churchill.

35.   Ibid., AFHQ, Algiers.

36.   Ibid.

37.   Ibid.

38.   Ibid.

39.   Ibid.

40.   Ibid.

41.   WO 106/3155, Eden.

42.   PREM 3/3/5, Eden.

43.   WO 106/3154, Eisenhower.

44.   CAB 120/501, AVM Sir John Linnell.

45.   Ibid., Eden.

46.   WO 106/3152, Churchill.

47.   Ibid., ACM Sir Charles Portal.

48.   Ibid., ACM Sir Arthur Tedder.

49.   Ibid.

50.   Ibid., General Sir Alan Brooke.

51.   Ibid., Churchill.

The Turkish Card

In 1920, the Treaty of Sevres was intended to bring about peace between Turkey who had fought on the side of the Kaiser in World War I, and the Allies. The Dardanelles were neutralized and held by Allied garrisons. Italy and Greece were given large parts of Asia Minor. AJP Taylor writes:

> The treaty was a dead letter from the start. The Greeks had taken Smyrna and then in 1922, Kemal Pasha struck against the Greeks and routed them. Smyrna fell to the Turks amid scenes of massacre. Lloyd George and Churchill responded with a call for action against Turkey. France and Italy were invoked as Allies. Canada and Australia refused. In point of fact, Kemal was only reclaiming Turkish territory. Lloyd George and Churchill thus ensured that the new Turkey would not be friendly to Great Britain.(1)

In November 1940, Winston Churchill was gravely concerned that the collapse of Greece, without any effort by Britain, would have a deadly effect on Turkey. Mr Churchill thought it would be agreeable to seize Rhodes and give it to Turkey: "The Turks would not be able to resist the offer and then they would be embroiled with Italy."(2) In the spring of 1942, both Romania and Hungary were providing the Germans with divisions to fight on the eastern front: "The Turkish President privately assured Franz von Papen, the German Ambassador to Turkey, that he was as convinced as ever of Germany's ultimate victory and was resolved to withstand British pressure on Turkey to abandon her neutrality."(3)

In the twelve-month period, November 1942-1943, the British Government conducted 128 staff talks with their Turkish counterparts. Indeed, in a short three-month period (16 August-15 November 1943), the British prepared twenty-two papers on the

Dardanelles question alone. Yet by March 1943, Churchill was advised of Turkish political difficulties in the event of British operations against the Dodecanese.

In November 1942, Churchill said that he wanted to bring pressure to bear on Turkey and: "Operate overland with the Russians into the Balkans."(4) As soon as the results of Alamein and TORCH were known, the Prime Minister (on 18 November 1942) sent a note to the British COS:

> A supreme and prolonged effort must be made to bring Turkey into the war in the spring. It should be possible to build up a powerful British land and air force to assist the Turks.(5)

The target date for operations in support of Turkey was projected for April or May. Equipment for the Turks was to come from Egypt and the United States. It would include tanks, anti-tank, and anti-aircraft guns. Meanwhile, the Prime Minister cautioned: "It would be a mistake to attack Rhodes and other islands until we have got Turkey on our side."(6) Thus, Churchill's assertions that he wished only to employ commandos in the Balkans is clearly discredited by his instructions to the COS to build up a powerful British force.

As 1942 drew to a close, arrangements were made to meet with the Turkish President, Ismet Inonu, at Adana, a town in Turkey close to the Syrian border. At Adana, Churchill outlined his program of military assistance to the Turks and dealt with his perceptions for a long-term treaty between the United States, Britain, Russia, and Turkey. The Turks were wary. The Turkish Prime Minister, Mr. Saracoglu, remarked: "All Europe was full of slavs and communists. All defeated countries would become Bolshevik and slav if Germany were beaten."(7) Churchill underscored the point, that Molotov had asked for a treaty by which the Baltic States would be regarded as Russian Provinces but stated: "We refused to agree to this."(8)

During the political discussions, military conversations were conducted by the British. These included the provision of materiel for the Turkish forces and the reinforcement of these forces by British units. Churchill then sent a letter to Stalin setting out what he felt had been achieved at Adana. Stalin's response was markedly cool:

> The international position of Turkey remains delicate. On the one hand Turkey has a treaty of neutrality and friendship with the USSR and a treaty of mutual assistance against aggression with Great Britain; on the other hand she has a treaty of friendship with Germany, signed three days before the German attack against the USSR. It is not clear to me how in the present circumstances Turkey thinks to combine her

obligation vis-a-vis the USSR and Great Britain
with her obligations vis-a-vis Germany.(9)

The Anglo-Turkish Agreement was formally ratified by the
Turkish Parliament on 12 May 1943, and the British military
assistance program given the code name HARDIHOOD. From reading
the wartime signals, there is little doubt that in the early
months of 1943, following the Russian successes in the Caucasus
and the British victory at Alamein, Churchill had set his sights
well beyond TORCH and the central Mediterranean. TORCH, he
said, "is no excuse for lying down during 1943, content with
descents on Sicily and Sardinia."(10)

The Prime Minister supported an Allied offensive against the
Italian Peninsula, but the area to be exploited was the Balkans
and for this, Turkey was the key. Churchill concluded later:
"I could have had Turkey in the war on our side before the end
of 1943. That this did not take place was due to the
unfortunate events in the Aegean later in the year."(11)

On 31 May, Mr. Churchill met with General Eisenhower and
Anthony Eden. Eden, at Churchill's request, commented on the
Turkish situation: "Knocking Italy out of the war would go a
long way towards bringing the Turks in."(12) Churchill was
concerned that Eden's turn of phrase might mislead the
Americans, and it was at this point that the Prime Minister said
that he "was not advocating sending an army into the Balkans now
or in the near future."

The Prime Minister was dissembling. He had previously called
for a supreme and prolonged effort; building up a powerful
British land and air force to assist the Turks. Even his
disclaimer is hedged by the qualifying words "now or in the near
future." There seems little doubt that had Churchill been
successful in opening a Turkish front in 1943, it could only
have been done at the expense of Allied plans for the assault on
the Italian Peninsula and on the cross-Channel invasion planned
for May 1944.

The Turkish Army Commander was convinced that, Turkey's policy
was to remain out of the war to the end. The Turkish Prime
Minister anticipated that, as a consequence of British pressure,
Germany was prepared to attack Turkey for preventive reasons.
On the 10 September, the JSM in Washington transmitted a report
to Roosevelt and Churchill which included the following estimate:
"The CCS think Turkey's future action will be guided more by the
course of events in the Russo-German theatre than by events in
the Balkans or Italy."(13)

With respect to the proposal that Rhodes and the Dodecanese be
recaptured by the Turks, the British COS felt that the political
difficulties were likely to prove insuperable. Staff talks
continued through November. Turkey had treaties with both
Germany and Britain. However, the Turks steadfastly refused to
provide Britain with the use of airfields to cover operations in
the Aegean at any time during the War.

From January to May 1943, some 16 million pounds sterling worth of equipment, other than gasoline, was carried to Turkey from the Middle East. These supplies formed the background to a more ambitious series of negotiations. From the end of January, when the Prime Minister and the CIGS visited Turkey, the Turks were aware that the Allies might later ask them to enter the War.

The British had already prepared their plans for this contingency but there is no evidence to suggest that the Americans had agreed to these plans. In April 1943, the CIC Middle East discussed plans in detail with the Turks at Ankara. In the event of Turkey entering the War, British support would be given in four separate phases:

- First phase: The provision of twenty-five RAF squadrons, mainly fighters, with AA artillery to protect their airfields and the provision of three anti-tank regiments.

- Second phase: The provision of twenty-five more RAF squadrons with the necessary AA artillery for the defense of their airfields.

- Third phase: The provision of two heavy AA regiments, two light AA regiments, and two more anti-tank regiments.

- Fourth phase: The provision of two armored divisions.(14)

It was obvious that the two armored divisions could not be maintained in Turkey unless the port of Smyrna (Izmir) had been opened. It was, therefore, essential first to control the Aegean. For this purpose, the British and the Turks discussed plans for capturing Rhodes, Kos, and some of the neighboring islands. As the Allied plans for Italy developed during August, the Joint Planning Staff reported that phase I of the plan to supply Turkey could not be carried out without a withdrawal of troops from the central Mediterranean, while the execution of phase II would involve the withdrawal of aircraft soon to be used for the strategic air offensive. At the same time Middle East Command was asked to keep all but one of its operational divisions in reserve for the Mediterranean Command.

In the middle of August, the COS concluded that Turkey should not be asked to join the Allies, but should be pressed instead to adjust its neutrality. The Prime Minister reluctantly agreed and at Quebec, the British stated: "The time was not ripe for Turkey to enter the war. Meanwhile, Turkey would be asked to interpret the Montreux Convention more strictly, to stop supplies of chrome to Germany, and to allow the British to make the first preparations for HARDIHOOD."(15)

One of the contributory arguments advanced by the JPS for

Turkey's continued neutrality was that the state of resources in the Middle East would no longer allow for operations against the Dodecanese, as a necessary preliminary to phase IV of HARDIHOOD. Given this appreciation, it is clear that there was no support for the operation and thus no point in taking a preliminary step into the Aegean. Notwithstanding the advice of the JPS, Churchill urged Wilson to secure Rhodes more quickly: "Here is a business of great consequence to be thrust forward by every means."(16) Meanwhile, in reference to the Dodecanese Islands, the JIC provided an assessment alluding to a plan of cover and deception, code name ZEPPELIN:

> Provided that we can persuade the enemy to believe that considerable forces and landing craft are being maintained in the eastern Mediterranean, it should be possible to contain enemy forces in the Balkans. Our chances of success would be increased if Turkey joined the Allies, but even if she refused one might still induce the enemy to fear the results of our continued infiltration."(17)

The enemy did, indeed, maintain significant divisional formations in the Balkans, essentially to protect his position in Hungary, Romania, and Greece. The JIC appreciation does not allude to Operation HARDIHOOD, or to the representations made by Churchill and Eden to induce Turkey to enter the War, eventualities which would be much more than "continued infiltration." As will be shown, there were no resources to mount HARDIHOOD in 1943, nor would any be available in 1944 unless there was to be a dramatic change in Allied strategy in favor of a Balkans front.

Only if the Germans had withdrawn from Italy would the British have been able to secure the necessary force for Turkey. We know that the fight to secure the Italian Peninsula involved a long and arduous campaign. One can imagine the catastrophic effect that would have resulted on the Italian front if Churchill had succeeded in poaching the landing craft, planes, and manpower he needed for HARDIHOOD. Even his less extravagant demands for ACCOLADE were deemed by Eisenhower to be "highly prejudicial" to the Italian campaign.

Two conclusions can be drawn in respect to this situation. First, without the political or military resources to mount HARDIHOOD, there was little to be gained by staging a preliminary round in the Dodecanese, since there were no British forces with which to follow up an initial incursion into the Aegean. Second, aware of the existence of the British plan to bring Turkey into the War, the Americans knew that the Prime Minister, contrary to his statements, would not be content with small scale commando type operations in the Balkans. Inevitably, a major thrust on a new Greco-Turkish front could only have been achieved by the redirection of men and materiel from the central Mediterranean and from forces assembled in England for OVERLORD. Perhaps the British read too much into the Adana strategy formulated in the spring of 1943. According to Erhman:

> Turkish foreign policy rested on a balance of power in eastern Europe. It, therefore, favored the traditional type of negotiated peace which would diminish Germany's influence before Russia's influence could be unduly exalted. But subsequent Allied successes seemed increasingly likely to sustain the Draconian measure of "unconditional surrender", and the consequent disappearance of a balance of power in eastern Europe.
>
> The Turks, afraid of an undisputed Russian dominance of the Balkans, now shrank from an undue loss of strength in a war whose objects they by no means wholeheartedly approved; while the British were less certain that they could spare the forces for a Turkish alliance. . .
> Whereas the capture of the Dodecanese had originally been designed to precede action by Turkey, action by Turkey was now required to secure possession of the Dodecanese.(18)

This analysis is borne out by the conversations between Anthony Eden and Mr. Numan, the Turkish Foreign Minister. The Turks were less than enthusiastic about giving support to British demands as is evidenced by Eden's own report of the proceedings. On the question of Turkish airfields, the COS thought more influence could be brought to bear on the Turks if the British asked the Russians to join in.

A meeting of the three Allied Foreign Ministers had begun in Moscow on 19 October. The British had two points to make: first, to persuade Turkey to grant the Allies the use of airfields immediately; and second, to bring Turkey into the war as soon as it would be practical to do so. The Russians, calculating that a belligerent Turkey would contain some ten German divisions, wanted the Turks to declare war on Germany by the end of the year. The Americans, fully aware of the diversion of resources that would follow such a step, preferred Turkey to remain neutral, and meanwhile, to lease the necessary airfields and communications to the British.

The British and Russian Foreign Ministers then proceeded to sign a three-point protocol, the gist of which was for Turkey to commit to enter the War by the end of 1943, and meanwhile to make available the Turkish airbases and such other facilities as the two Governments may agree are desirable. The Americans were not associated with this statement.   On 4 November, Eden left Moscow to meet the Turkish Foreign Minister and others in Cairo on the 5 November.   At 0227 hrs on the 6th, Eden cabled to his Prime Minister:

> We have had a long tough day with the Turks.   We have discussed both bases and Turkey's entry into the war this year.   Turks refused to accept that there is any real distinction between these two questions.   We used every argument we could but Numan repeated over and over again that if they let us use the bases the Germans could only conclude that Turkey had decided definitely to throw in her lot with the Allies.(19)

Numan showed himself deeply suspicious of the Russians: How could he be sure that Russia had no plans for penetration into the Balkans, and how could he tell what Russia's intentions towards Poland might be?   The first of these was of deep concern to Turkey.   Eden went on to say, that there had been no Turkish request for fulfillment of the Adana commitments.   However, Numan had asked for an assurance that Britain would continue with supplies.   Eden responded that, he could give no assurance about this until he knew the outcome of the present conversations.   Eden signaled to Churchill: "Discussion today was on several occasions pretty lively.   Tomorrow we propose to turn the heat on full.   I am not repeating this telegram to Moscow or Washington."(20)

The following day, Eden again met Numan and restated his views and requirements without being able to shift the Foreign Minister from his positions.   Numan also raised broader questions with respect to Turkey's role in the event that it entered the War.   He wanted to know whether Britain intended to mount operations in the Balkans.   Eden responded that he could not discuss Allied strategy at that point in time.   He said: "We ourselves considered that the best contribution the Turks could make was to play a passive role."   Numan replied: "Turkish public opinion would never agree to come into the war merely to play a passive part."(21)

The Turkish Foreign Minister then expressed the view that Eden might have brought more from Moscow to help him, such as a Russian assurance about Persia, Iraq, and the Balkans.   Eden responded: "We and Russia have our treaty with Persia and we both have pledged to withdraw from Persia after the war." Regarding the Balkans, Eden said: "I would not dream of going to our Russian allies and asking for a specific guarantee in respect of those countries."(22)   (Eastern Europe, with the exception of Greece and Turkey, has been dominated by the Russians ever since.)

Numan then hinted that the reason why the Soviets had ceased to press for a second front was because the Allies had given them a free hand in eastern Europe. Eden strongly repudiated this suggestion: "This sort of bargaining had never entered our heads." Numan inquired what more was expected of the Romanians who had already offered to surrender to the British. "Unconditional surrender to the Allies," replied Eden. According to Eden, Numan retorted warmly that, he "would never suggest to the Romanians that they should surrender to the Russians."(23)

Eden concluded the meeting with the Turkish Foreign Minister by saying that he had given Numan severe warning of the result which refusal to meet the British in either respect would have, not only on Anglo-Turkish relations but also on Turkey's relations with the Allies as a whole. He noted, with regret, his failure to obtain the use of airfields in support of Leros. The talks concluded on the 8 November.

The minutes of the Eden-Numan meeting shows that not only had Eden failed to obtain the use of Turkish airfields which were indispensable in Britain's desperate attempt to hold Leros, but that he had, by his threats, alienated the Turkish Foreign Minister to a considerable degree. There is certainly nothing in these minutes to suggest that Turkey was favorably disposed toward entering the War as a consequence of the Eden demarche. Three full days before the German assault on Leros, Eden was in a position to advise Wilson that support from the Turks would not be forthcoming. Sir Anthony Eden remained silent.

At the time, there were a number of problems in the Balkans, the Levant, and the Near East. These included American oil interests (which were becoming political problems of considerable importance); problems of opposing guerrilla factions in the Balkans; the Palestine problem; the possibility of bringing in greater Syria; the application of an Anglo-French financed agreement to the Levant states; and the problem of military supplies from the Middle East to Turkey. All these issues to some degree must have influenced Turkey's strategy, but none more deeply than its suspicions of Russia's intentions and her fear of, and possibly respect for, Germany.

Winston Churchill now put forward a watered-down version of the Eden-Numan meeting. On 10 November (two days before the German assault on Leros), the Prime Minister's office in London signaled to the Joint Staff Mission in Washington through the COS:

> Turkish Government is now considering the proposal put to them by the Foreign Secretary in Cairo last week that they should enter the war before the end of the year, and it seems highly desirable that we should consult with the Soviet government and agree upon the role that Turkey should adopt if, as we hope, she decides to come in.(24)

The role of Turkish forces would be: to secure the Dardanelles by holding Thrace and to open up a shorter supply route to Russia. Once Allied air forces were established in Anatolia, it would be possible to open the Aegean without delay. With regard to Rhodes and the Dodecanese, Churchill said:

> Although not operationally essential, it would clearly be desirable to clean up these islands as soon as possible and the idea that they should capture them should appeal to the Turks. We should have to be prepared to assist the Turks with naval and air forces and help to provide some amphibious equipment.(25)

The British proposed to deal with this matter, provided the political objections were not insuperable. The Turks were to say whether they were prepared to undertake the early capture of these islands on these conditions, and if they said they were unable to do so, the British intended to starve out the islands and occupy them later.

The action plan from the Prime Minister's office, which came two days before Leros was attacked, shows at last the truth behind the facade that Churchill had maintained for so long. Rhodes and the Dodecanese were not operationally essential to HARDIHOOD, and if they were to be captured, let the Turks undertake the task. Thus, the entire business of promoting ACCOLADE as a prerequisite to Turkey entering the war must come into question.

Had the Royal Navy or the CIC Middle East been aware of this rather brutal sloughing-off of their efforts to hold on to Leros, it is likely that they would have counseled against the reinforcement of the island's garrison and then made every effort to evacuate the troops, which had been there since the latter part of September.

On the other hand, the Allied incursion into the Dodecanese could have been a stratagem to keep the Germans occupied in the Balkans. Sacrifices could be made and would be acceptable particularly if they assisted in the attainment of major objectives in Italy.

On 12 November, a German battle group assaulted Leros by sea and by air. Six hundred paratroops of the Brandenburg Division emplaned in Rome flew to Athens and then on to Leros. They cut the island in two between Gurna Bay and Alinda Bay. Simultaneously, commandos made scramble landings. Heavy fighting ensued, and on 16 November, 234 Brigade HQ was captured and the British surrendered.

Five days after the fall of Leros, the Allies, and the British in particular, re-examined their Aegean options with reference to HARDIHOOD. These discussions took place at the Teheran Conference (EUREKA) in November, and at the Cairo conference

(SEXTANT) in November-December 1943.   At Teheran, the Prime
Minister said he wished to bring Turkey into the War: "It would
be possible to take the Dodecanese with two or three divisions
and thus, secure in the islands and in Turkey, to open the
passage to the Russian ports in the Black Sea."(26) (Both the
EUREKA and SEXTANT conferences came within a month after the
fall of Leros.)

Urged on by ghosts from the Dardanelles, Churchill considered
ways and means to induce Turkey to enter the War.   Josef Stalin
thought it a mistake to disperse forces by sending part to Turkey
and elsewhere and part to southern France for operation ANVIL.
Churchill intoned that he thought that the Soviet Government was
anxious to see Turkey enter the war.   Stalin responded by saying
that he was in favor: "We ought to take them by the scruff of
the neck, it would be worthwhile to take the islands."(27)
Ultimately he linked ANVIL to OVERLORD and dismissed Turkey's
participation [in the war] as a comparatively unimportant matter.

Again Churchill raised the question of landing craft for the
attack on Rhodes and to open the Aegean when Turkey entered the
War.   The CCS agreed that operations in the Aegean were entirely
dependent on the entry of Turkey into the War.   In any event, no
more landing craft were to be kept away from OVERLORD for the
specific purpose of operations in the Aegean.   The CCS were
finally unable to reach agreement on operations in the Aegean
until they received further instructions from President Roosevelt
and Prime Minister Churchill.   The CCS, followed by the two
political leaders, left for Cairo.   In Cairo, the problem of
assault shipping for the Aegean still had to be resolved.

The resolution of this problem had to face the competing
demands for OVERLORD as well as the Mediterranean, Indian, and
Pacific theatres of war.   The British COS recognized that
operations in the Aegean must conform to the requirements of
ANVIL and, therefore, placed less emphasis on the Aegean than
before.   In light of the programmed provision for assault
shipping, the COS recommended that Turkey should not enter the
War until mid-February 1944.

Churchill invited President Inonu of Turkey to join President
Roosevelt and himself on 4 December for discussions which were
to be held on successive days (4-7 December).   These discussions
turned on the extent of the damage which the Turks had to fear
from the Germans.   The Turks feared that the presence of 2,000
British technicians before the arrival of seventeen RAF
squadrons of fighters would provoke the Germans in advance of a
declaration of war. Professor Erhman writes:

> The Americans were no more enthusiastic than
> before about the Turkish alliance. When the CCS
> met on 3 December to consider in closed session
> the military implications of Turkey's entry into
> the war, the British minutes noted that there was
> an undercurrent of feeling throughout the

discussion against operations in the Aegean.(28)

After the fall of Leros, the Prime Minister, in concert with his Chiefs of Staff, worked out the details of a program of military aid to Turkey subject to a commitment by the Turks to enter the War. It was agreed that the measures would be divided into two stages: the first comprising a period during which British technicians (to the extent of some 2,000) and supplies would be introduced; the second, the arrival of seventeen RAF squadrons which would coincide with the declaration of war. If the Turks gave permission for the entry of the air squadrons, the Allies would open up the sea route from Egypt and the Levant, send in British anti-tank and armored units, and thus, bring into operation the plans already concerted. The final result appeared in a minute of the Prime Minister on 10 December:

> Air operations would be conducted against the enemy in the Aegean, while two divisions from the Middle East prepared to attack and garrison Rhodes. The attack would take place in March 1944, if enough assault shipping could be provided: if not, possibly Kos and Leros would be attacked."(29)

The preparations were given the code name SATURN and the capture of Rhodes was code-named HERCULES. The qualifying provision, to attack Kos and Leros, was a recipe for disaster, a characteristic of recent efforts by the British in the Dodecanese. With Rhodes still in German hands, the enemy would have been well positioned to bring elements of the GAF to bear against the newly arrived Allied fighter squadrons in Turkey. These squadrons would be without radar or an intercept network to plan both offensive and defensive sorties against Luftwaffe formations based in Greece and on Crete, Rhodes, and Kos. Thus, without Rhodes and Kos in British hands, sea routes and lines of communication would be no less perilous than before.

On 12 December, the Turks asked for more help and for more protection than had been offered so far. The Turkish Foreign Minister referred in adverse terms to the conversations in Cairo. The Turks were still apprehensive of German troop movements in Bulgaria and resented the "thrusting British approach." The British response was to offer more tanks, artillery, Spitfires, and medium bombers, provided the Turks adhered to the arrangements already made.

The Turks were also reminded that at Teheran, Stalin had expressed his willingness to declare war on Bulgaria should the need arise. A further demarche to Ankara by the British government and the government of the United States was also proposed. The Allied position was made very clear to the Turks. The measures were designed to ease the passage of earlier arrangements and not in any way to depart from them.

If the Turks refused, all British supplies would cease. The Turkish government refused to receive the British commanders from the Middle East and discussions were delayed.

The record clearly shows that, three weeks after the fall of Leros, the Prime Minister was still pushing hard to bring Turkey into the War and to secure Rhodes. Meanwhile, in December, the Allies were investing Monte Cassino while plans were proceeding to launch the attack on Anzio in January.

Further complications had risen. Following orders from the Combined Chiefs of Staff, AFHQ formulated a revised plan for operation ANVIL against southern France. The revised plan called for a heavier assault force to establish a broad, deep beachhead. Eisenhower informed the CCS that ANVIL had priority second only to OVERLORD and that it was imperative that assault shipping be provided, if necessary, from any source having lower priority than ANVIL. Moreover, the Americans were concerned about the provision of shipping for SHINGLE, the proposed landing at Anzio. Gordon A. Harrison, a US Military Historian writes:

> On considerable urging by Marshal Stalin, the Americans and British before leaving Teheran committed themselves to mounting OVERLORD with a supporting operation against the south of France during May 1944. It was clear that Marshal Stalin considered the two operations as a single, inseparable military undertaking. All other operations in the Mediterranean Stalin waved aside as diversion.
> He had no interest in any . . . [Mediterranean] operations other than those into Southern France. He admitted the desirability of getting Turkey into the war, but doubted that it could be done. In any case he felt that Turkey's participation was a comparatively unimportant matter. The important point was that he did not wish the Western Allies to contemplate any diversion whatsoever from OVERLORD. OVERLORD was the main question, not Turkey or Rhodes or the Balkans.(30)

The British COS recommended the cancellation of HERCULES against Rhodes and on Christmas Day, Churchill recognized with great regret that the Aegean and HERCULES must be ruled out. On 28 December, Roosevelt insisted that operations in the Aegean be sidetracked and the attack on Rhodes itself abandoned, at least until the attack on southern France had taken place. Clearly, this edict impacted not only the proposed assault on Rhodes (HERCULES) but also the provision of military aid to Turkey, (SATURN).

The call for landing ship tanks (LSTs) and assault shipping of all kinds continued and competed for priorities, with shortfalls everywhere. LSTs from Southeast Asia were required for the Mediterranean while many of the transports available in the Mediterranean were required to return to England for OVERLORD. In the face of these pressures, it is difficult to see just where the assault forces and materiel for HERCULES and SATURN were to be found.

Of necessity, the CIC Middle East reconsidered the feasibility of SATURN in the face of competing demands for manpower and shipping. Moreover, difficulties with the Turks, already in evidence, persisted. On 31 January, the British stopped all supplies to Turkey without explanation, and on 7 February, following a request from General Wilson, the Combined Chiefs of Staff released the forces hitherto earmarked for all plans affecting Turkey. Thus ended ACCOLADE (HANDCUFF and HERCULES) and HARDIHOOD (SATURN). Efforts to bring Turkey into the War were finally abandoned. When the post-war Greek Government was formed, the Dodecanese islands were ceded to Greece.

The reader may well contrast the makeshift efforts to capture Rhodes in September and October, with elements of the Tenth Indian Division, with the massive scale of operations, involving two first-class divisions to be carried out in late 1943 or early 1944. In light of the difficult struggle for the Italian Peninsula, the pending demands for operations ANVIL and OVERLORD and, even more critically, President Inonu's resolve to keep Turkey out of the War, the British Prime Minister's intention to embark on further seaborne adventures in the eastern Mediterranean becomes even more incomprehensible, unless it was nothing more than a stratagem, a "ruse de guerre."

By the end of September 1943, it was clear to the Turks and, no doubt, to Franz von Papen, the German Ambassador in Ankara, that while the situation still needed watching, it was unlikely that the Allies would be able to obtain Turkish support for a short-lived campaign in the eastern Mediterranean, or that Turkey would become a belligerent.

Following the overturn of Mussolini, Hitler did, indeed, express grave concerns with respect to the German position in the eastern Mediterranean. Earlier in the year (May 1943), the Italians had thirty-three divisions in Yugoslavia, Albania, Greece, and in the Aegean, while the Germans had one Corps of six divisions, later increased to eighteen divisions.

The incursion of 234 Brigade into the Dodecanese in September, undoubtedly gave the Germans cause for alarm. However, the necessary and sufficient condition to maintain the credibility of HARDIHOOD as a stratagem, or more remotely as a planned military operation to promote Turkey's entry into the War, fell away the moment the British failed to take Rhodes, followed then by the immediate fall of Kos. Professor AJP Taylor comments:

> The Turkish alliance was a will o' the wisp which
> Churchill pursued with unshakable constancy. It
> was probably fortunate that his dream never came

true. Turkish neutrality was a stronger barrier
against the Germans than her belligerence could
ever have been.(31)

It is true that Turkey's neutrality served as a block against
further German encroachment into the eastern Mediterranean and
the Levant. However, Sir Arthur Bryant, in his definitive war
history based on the diaries of Field Marshal Lord Alanbrooke,
says:

Goering and Admiral Raeder were pressing Hitler
to join Italy in attacking Britain's weakly held
bases in the Mediterranean and Middle East,
capture the Suez Canal and the Persian and Iraqi
oilfields, cutting the last link of the Balkan
States and Turkey with the West.(32)

Given this scenario, it is possible to place more credence on
Churchill's Balkans strategy. However, by early 1943, Allied
plans defining operational theatres in the central Mediterranean
and western Europe were in place. Hitler's strategy in the
Balkans was purely defensive. From this point on, the eastern
Mediterranean was not threatened by the Germans until the
British incursion into the Dodecanese.   Only then did the
Germans react, swiftly and successfully.

In April 1944, Turkey announced it was no longer neutral but a
pro-Allied country and would cease the vital chrome deliveries
to Germany within ten days. Privately, the Turkish Foreign
Minister apologized to von Papen explaining that his country had
been threatened with war by Russia and with blockade by the
Allies. By August, in the face of Russian military advances in
the Crimea, Romania had defected from the Tripartite Alliance,
and Turkey finally broke off diplomatic relations with Germany.

The Allies, by invading western Europe, had the dual
objectives of defeating Germany and blocking the Soviet Union
from moving into France. The crucible for the assault on Nazi
Germany was to be a cross-Channel invasion, bringing with it the
liberation of France and the Low Countries.

An incursion into the Balkans by the Allies would have served
not only to impair the primary military objective, the
destruction of Germany, but it would also have produced a
stronger Soviet influence in the Balkans than actually
transpired--namely, a Soviet presence in Greece and Turkey.
Moreover, if the Balkans rather than western Europe had become
the operational theatre for the second front, Russian forces
would have been free to maintain the momentum of their advance
through Nazi Germany into France, stopping only at the Channel
ports. Concomitantly, the postwar position of the Russians
throughout western Europe would have been significantly
enhanced and that of the Allies correspondingly weakened.

Cordell Hull, in a reference to eastern Europe, described it

as a: "Pandora's box of infinite trouble."(33)   Winston
Churchill did his best to open this box. Was the "Turkish Card"
an ace in the hole or was it a joker?   Did the British
Government seriously propose measures to bring about Turkey's
entry into the war or was it a stratagem, a plan of cover and
deception?

NOTES

1. AJP Taylor, English History, 1914-1945 (Oxford:
Oxford University Press, 1965), 190-191.

2. John Colville, The Fringes of Power (London: Hodder &
Stoughton, 1985),. 285.

3. Ibid., 287.

4. Winston S. Churchill, The Hinge of Fate, The Second
World War, 6 vols. (Boston: Houghton, Mifflin, 1950), 649.

5. Ibid., 697.

6. Ibid., 698.

7. Ibid., 710.

8. Ibid., 711.

9. Ibid., 715.

10. Ibid., 649.

11. Ibid., 716.

12. Ibid., 826.

13. Public Record Office, London, WO 3154.

14. John Erhman, Grand Strategy, vol. 5 (London: Her
Majesty's Stationery Office, 1956), 90.

15. Ibid., 91.

16. Winston S. Churchill, Closing the Ring (Boston:
Houghton, Mifflin, 1951), 204.

17. Anthony Cave Brown, Bodyguard of Lies (New York:
Harper & Row, 1975), 391.

18. Erhman, Grand Strategy, 90, 100.

19.   WO 106/3154.

20.   Ibid.

21.   Ibid.

22.   Ibid.

23.   Ibid.

24.   Public Record Office, London, PREM 3/3/3.

25.   Ibid.

26.   Erhman, Grand Strategy, 174.

27.   Ibid., 175.

28.   Ibid., 194.

29.   Ibid., 195.

30.   Harrison, GA, "Cross-Channel Attack", United States Army in World War II, The European Theatre of Operations (Washington, DC: Department of the Army, 1951), 125.

31.   Taylor, English History, 522.

32.   Sir Arthur Bryant, Turn of the Tide (New York: Doubleday, 1957), 194.

33.   David Eisenhower, Eisenhower at War, 1943-1945 (New York: Random House, 1986), 16.

Cover and Deception

Churchill said that: "In war-time, truth is so precious that she should always be attended by a bodyguard of lies."(1) In World War II, the British and Americans carried on a clandestine war of intelligence and counterintelligence involving a variety of agencies that specialized in covert operations, including espionage, sabotage, and deception to confuse the enemy.

Churchill had established a secret bureau within his personal headquarters to plan stratagems to deceive Hitler. Meanwhile, the British Intelligence Service (MI6) joined with its American counterpart, the Office of Strategic Services (OSS). Both were under control of the Joint Intelligence Committee (JIC), which reported to the US Joint Chiefs of Staff and the British Chiefs of Staff.

The primary purpose of the overall deception policy was to mislead Hitler about Allied strategy and military operations, particularly with respect to those planned for the Mediterranean and western Europe. At the Casablanca Conference in January 1943, two plans were formulated. Anthony Cave Brown has written extensively on two key stratagems used in World War II, one of which was central to the war in the eastern Mediterranean:

> The first was COCKADE, which was intended to contain the maximum enemy forces in western Europe and the Mediterranean area and thus discourage their transfer to the Russian front. The second was ZEPPELIN, whose objective was to deceive Hitler into believing that, at the end of the Tunisian campaign, the Allies would not invade Sicily and Italy but rather would invade Greece and southern France.(2)

What was the truth behind the reality of Allied operations in the Aegean in September 1943? Were these intended to be live operations or were they a feint, a stratagem designed to draw German forces away from the main battlefronts? To whom did Churchill speak? What did he say, and what were the reactions of the listeners, especially, Stalin and Roosevelt? Crucial questions center around the actions taken by the Prime Minister: What initiatives did he approve? What military commitments did he make, what was the effect on Allied perceptions on the course of the War? And what were the German's likely reactions to the prospect of having to fight in the Balkans?

The statements made and actions of President Roosevelt, Prime Minister Churchill, General George C. Marshall, General Dwight Eisenhower, ACM Sir Arthur Tedder, and General Sir Alan Brooke have been identified and elaborated upon in this account. The reaction of the Turkish government to Eden's demarche has been critically reviewed, and mention has been made of Hitler's concern for the southeastern flank of his "Fortress Europe."

On the face, it does seem that both Churchill and Eden set considerable store by the British agreement reached with the Turks at Adana. In the summer of 1943, the Germans did reinforce their garrisons in Yugoslavia, Romania, and Greece, and there is evidence to show that Hitler regarded the Aegean islands as, "the barbicans of southeastern Europe."(3)

The British Prime Minister's attempts to secure from President Roosevelt the commitment of a major Allied force in the eastern Mediterranean, and the deployment of agents and commandos or a tactical force as a "ruse de guerre" were all implicit in Churchill's actions. None of the options were mutually exclusive, and the possibility of Churchill's strategy being nothing more than "cover and deception" cannot be ruled out. However, the evidence suggests that his actions were much more than a stratagem to keep German forces tied down in the Balkans.

In outlining the cause and effect of operations in the Aegean, we have tried to focus on provocative questions that, tangentially at least, are linked to the issue of cover and deception. The problem in discerning the truth behind the Aegean venture is in attaching the proper weight to Churchill's intentions and the impact of the strategy that he so doggedly pursued in order to set the "Balkans ablaze."

The availability of mineral resources (copper, bauxite and chrome) in the Balkans, and, in particular, protection of the Ploesti oilfields were all matters of concern to the German leader. With the collapse of the Italian garrisons in the Balkans, Hitler felt a greater concern: "Communist uprisings might lead to the worst nightmare of all, to exposing the German southern flank."(4) Did the Allies fool Hitler as to their intentions and actions in the eastern Mediterranean? All that can be said with certainty is that Allied intentions were never matched by commensurate actions. Turkey did not permit the Allies use of her airfields in Anatolia, nor did she enter the war.

Anthony Cave Brown provides a fascinating reconstruction of a ruse, first suggested by Lieutenant-Commander Ewen Montagu (a member of British Naval Intelligence), which attempted to fool the Germans into believing that the Allies would attack in Greece rather than in Sicily. Operation MINCEMEAT was the code name used for a plan to drop a corpse into the sea, dressed as a Marine officer and suitably equipped with false operational papers. This stratagem later became famous in Montagu's book The Man Who Never Was.(5)

It is significant to note that operations in the Aegean took place in September three months after the Allied assault on Sicily, and shortly after the Allied landings at Salerno. It is, therefore, unlikely that the Germans would then consider the Dodecanese to be the main thrust for a new offensive. The Allied commitment of major forces to the Italian Peninsula was obvious enough; a commitment to the Aegean less so. The stratagem became quite implausible after Allied forces had been aligned for a thrust in the central Mediterranean.

Increasing efforts were made by Winston Churchill to draw upon landing craft, P-38 fighter planes, troops, and logistical support from AFHQ in Algiers. The concerned responses by Roosevelt, Marshall, Eisenhower, Tedder and Alan Brooke have been documented throughout all phases of operations in the Aegean. The planned scale of Allied forces has been variously described; earlier attempts involving a first class division to take Rhodes, the deployment of an infantry brigade group on three small islands in the Dodecanese and ultimately a two divisional scenario. Should the actual commitment be regarded as a red herring, to confuse the enemy, or as a determined attempt to secure a bridgehead into the Balkans?

As a battle group, 234 Brigade was unable to hold Kos and Leros, while Rhodes could never have been captured by a single brigade or even the 10th Indian Division. The magnitude of Allied sea power in support of operations in the Aegean was, however, not insignificant. More than one hundred ships of the Royal Navy, (with Greek and Polish naval elements) were sent into action; virtually the entire British Mediterranean Fleet (except battleships and aircraft carriers) was exposed to continual bombing attacks by the GAF in the Aegean approaches.

Allied logistical support for military assistance to Turkey would have made heavy demands on Allied resources, correspondingly depleting men and materiel needed for operations on other fronts. If the British Foreign Minister had been successful in his demarche with his counterpart, Mr. Numan, calling upon Turkey to enter the War (c. February-March 1944), it is difficult to perceive just who among the Allies would have been willing or able to procure the weapons and troops, and then to send them into the eastern Mediterranean, when the Allies were already committed to fight in Italy and in western Europe.

The Prime Minister's political initiative to deploy a force

into the Aegean did call for a heavy commitment and it did produce a disaster. This was the effect, whether as a stratagem or as a military operation to induce Turkey to enter the war. It amounted to the same thing. Churchill described his Aegean strategy as the most acute difference he ever had with General Eisenhower. Dr Pogue recalls a discussion in Cairo on 24 November, one week after the fall of Leros:

> Churchill called in the Combined Chiefs of Staff. Almost at once he turned the conversation to the Rhodes operation, on which he had been unable to sell Marshall the previous evening. Although not strong for the operation, the British COS supported their leader. As Marshall remembered the discussion: "All the British were against me."
>
> It got hotter and hotter. Finally Churchill grabbed his lapels, his spit curls hung down and he said: "His Majesty's Government can't have his troops standing idle. Muskets must flame!" I said, "God forbid if I should try to dictate but, not one American soldier is going to die on that goddamned beach! The others were horrified, but they didn't want the operation and were willing for me to say it."(6)

One cannot be sure, but in all probability, Churchill was serious in his intention to capture Rhodes as a preliminary to bringing Turkey into the War. To the extent that his rhetoric served to unsettle Hitler, a stratagem was an acceptable alternative, and it may have been "Hobson's Choice," since he had no force with which to capture the island. As Major-General David Lloyd Owen has written in the foreword to The Aegean Mission, "there are still many questions remaining unanswered and on which judgments ultimately will be made."(7) The engagement of more than one hundred warships in the narrow waters of the Aegean Sea was, in itself, a major commitment of force; certainly an expensive stratagem!

NOTES

1. Anthony Cave Brown, Bodyguard of Lies (New York: Bantam Books, 1976, published by arrangement with Harper & Row, 1975), 10.

2. Ibid., 275.

3. Ibid.

4. Ibid., 287.

5.   Ewen Montagu, The Man Who Never Was, War Classics series, (London: Evans, 1966).

6.   Forrest C. Pogue, George C. Marshall: Organizer of Victory, 1943-1945 (New York: The Viking Press, 1973), 307.

7.   Jeffrey Holland, The Aegean Mission (Westport, Conn.: Greenwood Press, 1988), xiv.

Turning Points

The terms of the Italian surrender, which came into effect on 9 September, stipulated that all Italian armed forces personnel should take up arms against the Germans. Yet one might ask, what incentive had the Italians for taking such a step? Moreover, in the face of the British Eighth Army's experience with Italian troops in the western desert, how realistic were Allied expectations that these troops would perform effectively? To make such support a prerequisite for success in pending Aegean operations was nothing more than a pious hope.

Italy had been fascist throughout the inter-war years. Psychologically she was attuned to Benito Mussolini and the prevailing fascist ethos. For three years, Italy had been Germany's ally, and for three years, the British had maintained propaganda against the Italians. The Allies had brought down Mussolini and, along with him the Italian fascist empire. A new status of "co-belligerent" was unlikely to bring about the restoration of Italy's former possessions in Libya or in the Dodecanese.

The British had fought Italian divisions in the desert and had roundly defeated them. The Italians had been in the war for three years, seemingly with no value or gain. Following the coup d'etat and the execution of Mussolini, their troops did not relish the prospect of taking on the Wehrmacht, for whom they understandably felt a wary respect. The Italian soldiers had given it their "best shot," never mind that it was a poor performance by British standards: "Time to go home, Guiseppe, al diavolo con gli Ingelsi."

The intrinsic worth of operations in the Aegean was never recognized, save by the advocates--the Prime Minister and a few ambitious planners--who did no more than sketch out the scenarios. Force 292 was never able to match objectives with resources if only because the former were constantly changing, while resources were never sufficient to match ephemeral objectives. HARDIHOOD was never an intrinsic part of ACCOLADE, or vice versa. Moreover, as a limited plan, ACCOLADE had very little merit. The capture of Rhodes would still have left Luftwaffe fighter groups on Crete and in Greece. As the tide of war, which had already moved westward, continued on its course, a British garrison on Rhodes would have remained there, isolated from the main stream of events. Occupation of the island, in and of itself, was never enough to induce Turkey to enter the War.

The rhetoric used by the British Prime Minister served merely to reinforce the Americans in their view that an Aegean gamble would vitiate the force of approved plans and agreed strategies. Churchill pressed on with his customary disregard for a consensus: "Here is a business of great consequence. This is the time to play high. Improvise and dare."(1) High-sounding phrases were shortly replaced by more sombre ones: "We face a most vexatious disaster in this part of the world."(2) As with all prima donnas, the Prime Minister sought to blame someone else for his own misfortunes. Alluding to the Americans he said: "I am fighting with my hands tied behind my back."(3)

We have seen from published accounts that Wilson's intention in August 1943 was to mount a "quick" ACCOLADE--an assault against Rhodes with one infantry division plus supporting arms. At this point, the occupation of Kos, Leros, or Samos was not necessarily a part of the plan. Rhodes was the key. While it appeared that tacit approval had been given to this plan by virtue of some support from General Marshall, it is clearly shown that, by 12 August, Eisenhower, together with Alexander and Tedder, had decided against the plan, saying: "ACCOLADE should be abandoned."(4)

This is the first point where the Aegean business could have been put on the back burner or abandoned. Subsequently, we see agreement among both the British and the Americans to stick with the decisions made at TRIDENT. The CIC Middle East, General Wilson, on 31 August, reported: "Any enterprise against Rhodes except as an unopposed walk-in is now impossible."(5) In light of the CIC's appreciation, it is evident that he had bitten off more than he could chew, or at least was at the point of doing so. This is the second occasion when the Aegean undertaking could have been aborted.

We have seen how, on the night of 9-10 September, Major The Earl Jellicoe, SBS [Staff Officer to Colonel DJT Turnbull, Chief of the British Mission to Rhodes, (Rodell)], met with Admiral Campioni. We know that the Admiral was either unwilling or unable to make any commitment to assist a British landing against the Germans. In any event, General Scaronia was taken prisoner by the German General Klemann and the Regina Division attacked by German troops on 11 September. This presented a third, and compelling, reason to abort Allied operations in the Aegean.

Based on the performance of Italian troops in the western

desert and, more cogently, the Allies' knowledge of the prowess of the German troops, it is incredible that anyone would believe the Italians could round up 7,000 German troops, an Assault Division on Rhodes. Moreover, even with Campioni's full support, the scenario shows 234 Brigade trying to disembark in the teeth of an alert German garrison three times their strength in numbers and much more deadly in their ability to fight close quarter combat. It is also an inescapable fact that one or two squadrons of Spitfires would have lasted but a short while in the face of ten times that number of Me 109s.

On 13 September, Churchill, en route to Halifax, signaled Wilson: "The capture of Rhodes by you at this time with Italian aid would be fine contribution to the general war."(6)   Once again this was an example of the Churchillian formula: some minor insight coupled with a major inspirational plea. On 14 September, Wilson started to provide garrisons for Kastellorizo, Kos, Leros and Samos. An incredible decision was then made. General Wilson, on 21 September, submitted proposals to capture Rhodes to the British Chiefs of Staff.

Churchill seemed to dismiss both the swift action taken by the German Commander on Rhodes to secure his position, and the fact that Wilson's depleted Middle East reserve force (the balance of Tenth Indian Division) could never secure the objective. The reader will recall that by 25 September, the three islands (Kos, Leros and Samos) were each garrisoned by an infantry battalion; thus, the major part of 234 Brigade was dispersed among the smaller islands, but not on Rhodes.

On 1 October, the British COS authorized General Wilson, in consultation with General Eisenhower, to capture Rhodes before the end of October. For this purpose, Wilson was to use the partly equipped Tenth Indian Division which, as we have seen, was without 234 Brigade. There is no doubt that Churchill's intention was to join the forces and shipping from the central Mediterranean to augment this emasculated division; the only infantry division under Wilson's Middle East Command.

On 3 October, Kos was assaulted by a German battle group and fell in a day. This is the fourth point where any further operations in the Aegean could have been aborted. Rhodes was a non-starter, and now Kos was gone, leaving no airfields or local air cover for Leros and Samos. On 10 October, the Allied Commanders in Chief at La Marsa stated bluntly that: "If Rhodes is not captured and held, there is no chance to defend and maintain Leros and Samos. We must concentrate on the Italian campaign. ACCOLADE must be postponed."(7) This is the fifth point in time when the Aegean venture could have been aborted or at least postponed.

Eden had met Wilson in Cairo. He sent a signal to Churchill: "We are in no doubt we should hold on to Leros."(8) This was the position on 12 October, one month to the day before Leros was, in its turn, assaulted by a superior German force. The truth is that to maintain a position in the Dodecanese and thus exert some influence over Turkey, it would have been necessary to capture and hold both Kos and Rhodes. These were the two islands with airfields.

Despite the conclusions of the La Marsa Conference, General Wilson had continued to reinforce Leros and Samos. This was not called into question from London. By 12 October every informed commander had made his appreciation on the Aegean situation. General Sir Alan Brooke, ACM Sir Arthur Tedder, ACM Sir Charles Portal, Admiral Sir Andrew Cunningham, and many others all felt that the Allies should cut their losses; Leros simply could not be held without air cover, and in all events, it was probably not worth the effort. Churchill, Eden, and General Wilson disagreed: Leros must be held at all costs.

It is from this point on that the Royal Navy lost HMS ECLIPSE, DULVERTON, HURWORTH and PANTHER; HHMS/M KATSONIS, HMS/M SIMOON and TROOPER; and various motor torpedo boats (MTBs) and coastal craft. Severe damage was done to four cruisers, four destroyers, and four submarines: HMS AURORA, CARLISLE, PENELOPE, SIRIUS; ADRIAS, HURSLEY, PENN, ROCKWOOD; HMS/M TORBAY, UNRIVALLED, UNSEEN and UNSPARING. A total of 32 ships sunk or crippled. (HMS INTREPID and HHMS QUEEN OLGA were sunk in September).

In the conversations between Eden and the Turkish Foreign Minister in Cairo (5-8 November), it was made clear that Turkey would not permit the British use of its airfields to cover the Dodecanese. Following the fall of Kos, one military appreciation after another cautioned against any further commitment in the Aegean. These appreciations were made a month before the German assault on Leros.

The Leros garrison continued to hold on in less than splendid style, at the end of very perilous lines of communications and without close air support, while the Royal Navy absorbed prohibitive losses in its attempts to supply the island. This token and fleeting lodgment in the Dodecanese scarcely served to convince Turkey of the Allies' latent capability to mount operation HERCULES or the even more ambitious SATURN. The Germans had polished off Kos in short order and, on 12 November, using their Kos assault force, successfully attacked Leros. This, however, was not the end of Churchill's Aegean aspirations. Within five days following the fall of Leros, he was urging support for a new ACCOLADE (HERCULES).

It is clear that, without Rhodes and with the fall of Kos, the British foothold in the Aegean was extremely precarious. Furthermore, it does seem that the force for HARDIHOOD (or SATURN) was a phantom force. This was surely a ruse de guerre unless the Americans were willing to supply virtually the entire assault force and, in so doing, commit themselves to a Balkans front. Certainly, there is nothing in the order of battle to show how the British intended to conjure up fifty fighter squadrons, two armored divisions, and numerous regiments of artillery to support Turkey in November 1943 or in February

1944. Unless this deficiency can be refuted, the entire plan to bring Turkey into the War must be regarded, at best, as a stratagem and, at worst, as a ploy by Churchill, possibly to expiate for his failure at Gallipoli in World War I.

This question deserves closer examination in order to understand the reasoning behind the obsessive conduct on the part of the Prime Minister and the planners who may have encouraged him to pursue such a poorly conceived course of action in the first place. The conventional wisdom was to concentrate Allied resources in the Mediterranean on the Italian front and to build up for OVERLORD. We know that the displacement of even six Lightning squadrons, bomber groups, and shipping from the central Mediterranean to the Aegean was viewed with dismay by Eisenhower, Alexander, Tedder, and Brooke.

President Roosevelt was greatly concerned about the corrosive effect on Allied air and land forces in Italy that would result from major operations in the Aegean, and by extension, involvement with Turkey. However, there was never a Turkish commitment to enter the War in 1943, nor to provide the British with airfields. Furthermore, the record shows how, by maintaining a presence in the Dodecanese, the British lost so much for no value or gain other than to kill 2,000 or 3,000 Germans. Certainly there was no strategic gain.

Offsetting this effort, the British task force captured the attention of the enemy for a short time resulting in the diversion of GAF units to the eastern Mediterranean. On the other hand, the British, in turn, had to divert from the central Mediterranean air and naval resources that might have been better employed on the Italian front. Most significantly, the Aegean venture did not improve the Allies' position in the Balkans generally and it worsened their position vis-a-vis Turkey. What then, was the purpose of the stratagem if, indeed, it was nothing more than that?

The most that can be said is that Hitler felt threatened in the Balkans. He believed that the seven British divisions earmarked for OVERLORD were to be used in support of a belligerent Turkey. It is true that, following the surrender of Italy, the enemy reinforced divisional strengths in the Balkans from eight divisions in March to eighteen by 10 July, and it is also true that had Turkey entered the War, the enemy would have been forced to divert additional divisions to neutralize the effects of major operations in the Balkans.

Russian estimates that the Germans would have committed ten additional divisions to the Turkish front are speculative. This commitment would only have come about had the Turks mounted full-scale offensive operations, backed up by significant British support. Clearly, with twenty-eight divisions in the Balkans, the Germans would then have assembled a formidable force calling for a corresponding commitment by the Allies. This was the very problem the Americans sought to avoid because of the calamitous effect it would have had upon the previously agreed strategy for Italy and northwestern Europe.

What conclusions can be drawn from these events? The deception strategy (ZEPPELIN) was designed to maintain belief in an Allied threat to the Balkan theatre of operations (Hungary, Yugoslavia, Romania, Albania, Bulgaria, Greece and Turkey). Yet, deployment of 18 German divisions in this region was essentially a force designed to protect the Romanian oilfields, to neutralize Yugoslav and Greek partisans, and to pacify the entire region. It was not a defense force to repel an Allied invasion in the Balkans.

Arguably, a decision by Turkey to enter the War would have served to shackle German forces otherwise committed in Italy, or soon to be engaged in Normandy. However, as we have seen, the Turks were never convinced that it was in their best interest to become embroiled with Germany and perhaps later with the Soviets. The key point remains, the adverse impact of opening a Turkish front on all other agreed Allied operations in the central Mediterranean and in western Europe. The British operation in the Aegean was essentially sacrificial, as was the Dieppe Raid in 1942.

From his own statements, it would appear that Winston Churchill really hoped to open a Balkans front in preference to an Allied assault in northwestern Europe. His intention went well beyond "cover and deception." However, in either event, the assignment of a single infantry brigade into the Dodecanese, without first ensuring the capture of Rhodes, was intolerable and insupportable--a vain gesture, soon dispelled by superior force of arms.

Conclusions on the British incursion into the Aegean in the autumn of 1943 provide reasoned argument and elaboration on the politics, planning, and execution of the operation. The principal points of consideration include: Hitler's concern and the German reaction to the British presence in the islands; the notion of support by Italian troops; the failure to capture Rhodes; Churchill's insistence on maintaining the Aegean effort after Kos had fallen; his attempts to pre-empt Allied plans in the central Mediterranean and northwestern Europe in order to open a second front through Turkey; and the steadfast refusal by Roosevelt and Eisenhower to support the Prime Minister's strategy in the eastern Mediterranean.

Churchill never seemed to realize that the issue was not the nine landing craft, from those earmarked for OVERLORD, for which he had asked. The real issue was the maintenance of OVERLORD and to a lesser extent ANVIL as the primary and secondary objectives for the assault on "Fortress Europe.". Referring to ANVIL, AJP Taylor has said: "The Americans proposed it in order to prevent any Churchillian action in the eastern Mediterranean. Churchill agreed to it because it would keep landing craft in the Mediterranean and away from the Channel."(9) ANVIL, renamed DRAGOON, was launched on 15 August, 1944, from Marseille and St Tropez. It was destined to become a ten division thrust by American and French forces up the Rhone Valley in support of OVERLORD.

NOTES

1.   CJC Molony et al., The Mediterranean and Middle East, vol. 5, History of the Second World War (London: Her Majesty's Stationery Office, 1973), 538.

2.   Public Record Office, London, PREM 3/3/5.

3.   Ibid.

4.   Ibid.

5.   Molony, The Mediterranean, 537.

6.   Winston S. Churchill, Closing the Ring (Boston: Houghton, Mifflin, 1951), 114.

7.   Ibid.

8.   Ibid.

9.   Ibid.

10.   AJP Taylor, English History, 1914-1945 (Oxford: Oxford University Press, 1965), 573.

Conclusions on the Aegean Venture

In the official history of the Second World War, Molony writes:
"Hitler decided to defend the Aegean in order to deny to the
Allies island stepping-stones towards the southeast mainland; to
counter Allied influence upon Turkey; and to block Allied
attempts, in which Turkey might connive, to create a supply
route to Russia via the Marmara and Black Sea."(1)

There was a real chance of island prizes being obtained at
small cost, the more so if the Italian garrisons rallied stoutly
behind the Allies. British plans were, in fact, based on this
assumption. However, it became clear shortly after the
surrender of Italy that the Italians were not disposed to fight
seriously against the Germans. It was also evident by the end
of September that the Germans were reinforcing the Aegean:
"Support by the Italians was the essential prerequisite; without
it, General Wilson's tactical plan was clearly inadequate to the
task. It was at this juncture when the decision to withdraw
from the Dodecanese might well have been taken."(2)

The British position in the Aegean turned upon the occupation
of Rhodes. With occupation of the island went control of the
air, the ability to cover naval movement, and the ability to
make secure the advantages gained from the Italian collapse.
However, it was established in mid-August that a full-scale
assault against the island could not be mounted from the
resources available in the Middle East. Moreover, it was
confirmed that nothing should be done to prejudice operations
in Italy.

This decision was never allowed to crystallize into a firmly
established maxim. After the failure to acquire Rhodes in the
period immediately following the Italian collapse, the CIC
Middle East proceeded to act in the Aegean in the hope that the
island might fall into Allied hands: "General Maitland Wilson
never seemed to have despaired of assistance from the central
Mediterranean."(3) The British Prime Minister would not
tolerate what he regarded as a setback to his ambitions in the

eastern Mediterranean.   Ultimately, he was to attribute the
blame to others:

> There are two causes for these misfortunes. The
> artificial line of division between east and west
> in the Mediterranean, absolving Western commanders
> who have the forces of all responsibility for
> vital interests at stake in the east. The second
> cause is the shadow of OVERLORD. We are now
> faced with the prospect that a fixed date for
> OVERLORD will continue to wreck and ruin the
> Mediterranean campaign; that our affairs will
> deteriorate in the Balkans and that the Aegean
> will remain firmly in German hands.(4)

The Prime Minister was being his petulant self. Allied Force
Headquarters in Algiers was accountable for all operations in
the Mediterranean. The Western commanders were responsible for
major amphibious operations (Sicily, Salerno, and Anzio), in
respect to which a complex range of logistics and tactical
movements had been carefully drawn up. Operations in the
eastern Mediterranean were not recognized as having significant
strategic merit, least of all at the expense of the Italian
campaign, which was linked to planned operations in southern
France (ANVIL) and, by extension, to OVERLORD.
Having failed to wrest shipping, aircraft, and troops from
AFHQ Algiers, the British Prime Minister then sought to blame
those responsible for OVERLORD, since they were commandeering
the resources he needed for ACCOLADE. Winston Churchill's
petulant reference to "wreck and ruin" has nothing whatever to
do with the Mediterranean campaign as it related to Sicily,
Sardinia, Corsica, or Italy. The vital interests at stake in
the east were essentially his own perceptions: to take control
of the Aegean.
The fact that Middle East Command was now within a minor
sphere of operations was an inescapable fact of life; the center
of gravity for operations in the Mediterranean had moved from
Cairo to Algiers. The Middle East, however, continued to figure
prominently in British strategic planning, due solely to the
Prime Minister's insistence that ACCOLADE merited everyone's
attention and that Allied shipping, troop, and air dispositions
should be made accordingly. As noted, operation ANVIL had by
now been expanded to ten divisions, and this commitment of force
and landing craft finally closed out the Aegean/Turkish option.
Possession of the Dodecanese did not materially affect
Turkey's decision to enter the War, and the failure by British
forces to capture and hold Rhodes did not significantly alter
the situation in Yugoslavia or in Greece, both beset by
political problems. In any event, the Germans evacuated the
Aegean in August 1944. Churchill's criticism of the American

commanders concerning shipping for OVERLORD is also argumentative. The assault shipping which he demanded for ACCOLADE was always needed for operations in the central Mediterranean and, ultimately, for ANVIL and the cross-Channel invasion. AJP Taylor, in a reference to operations in southern France (ANVIL), says of Churchill:

> He stirred up General Sir Henry Maitland Wilson, the Commander in the Middle East, to seize the Italian islands in the Aegean. Wilson obeyed. The Americans refused to authorize reinforcements. The British forces were overwhelmed by the Germans. Most of them were taken prisoner. This was not only an unnecessary misfortune. It shattered another of Churchill's dreams: that of bringing Turkey into the war.(5)

After the fall of Kos (the precursor to the attack on Leros), it might have been calculated that an evacuation of Leros and Samos could have been achieved with precisely the same effort as their essential reinforcement, in addition, so suitable an opportunity to evacuate the islands would not come again: "At this juncture, a week was lost before the La Marsa conference again established the fact that, the capture of Rhodes was impractical in the light of our Allied strategy. During this interval (3-10 October), evacuation of Leros and Samos was not considered."(6)

Despite the conclusions of the La Marsa Conference, General Wilson continued to reinforce these two islands. This was not called into question from London. There was further delay awaiting the arrival of Anthony Eden in Cairo. Thus, there was an interval of four days between acceptance of the conclusions of the La Marsa Conference and the Foreign Secretary's recommendation that Leros should be held. This recommendation was made eleven days after the fall of Kos: "The fate of Leros was befogged by the consideration of the verdict on the projected operations against Rhodes and Kos."(7)

The Prime Minister, in effect, did not adhere to his acceptance of the conclusions of the La Marsa Conference and, although he at no time overruled General Wilson, it must be accepted that his personal view had a considerable influence upon the course of events. The CICs Middle East, who made the decision that these activities should continue after the Rhodes operations were abandoned, were handicapped by the delays which preceded the major decisions taken at La Marsa and Cairo on 10 and 14 October respectively.

On 11 October, after Kos had fallen, and in reply to questions from Whitehall as to the fate of British garrisons that had recently been sent up to Leros and Samos, General Wilson felt that, having sent the forces there, it would now be very difficult to bring them back; that their retention in the area

was not an impossibility, given Turkish aid; and that their
continued presence there would be an irritation to the enemy,
which might cause them to direct and hold forces in the Aegean
that might otherwise be sent to France or Russia. Barrie Pitt,
a military historian, makes a perceptive comment on this precise
point:

> Why he [Wilson] thought Turkish aid should
> suddenly become available in such form and
> substance as to protect British troops under
> threat of destruction is difficult to see; and a
> superficial knowledge of German military attitudes
> in general and Generalleutnant Mueller's in
> particular should have told him that neither were
> likely to put up with irritations for a moment
> longer than they had to.

> The Royal Navy was the first to feel the shock of
> the German reactions. Many years afterwards, one
> of the cruiser captains said that these losses,
> sustained in what he called the most pointless
> campaign of the war, brought him and his fellow
> commanders nearer to mutiny than any other
> situation during their naval careers, and only
> the plight of the unfortunate soldiers on Leros
> took them back into such dangerous areas again.(8)

It can only be imagined what a frightful strain was thrown on
the crews and, in particular, on the captains of Royal Navy
ships. Similarly, the crews of the small ships and boats who
operated throughout the Dodecanese under equally hazardous and
arduous conditions frequently went without sleep or respite from
bombing attacks. The crews facing one emergency after another
incurred heavy losses.

The security of Leros and Samos could not be guaranteed without
the use of Turkish airfields, whether or not this security
involved the recapture of Kos. Although this was recognized in
October, it was not until 6 November, that the Turkish reaction
became clear. This interval was due to the Moscow Conference
and the decision to await the arrival of the Foreign Secretary's
return to Cairo. It might have been realized that some time
would elapse before the Turkish attitude became known, and in
these circumstances, it was probably fatal to accept the
inevitable delay.

German naval units operating in the Aegean were far fewer than
those employed by Britain. The success of German arms against
the Royal Navy was due to a number of causes: enemy aircraft
accounted for 46 percent of Britain's naval losses, 20 percent
were due to gunfire and depth charges, 12 percent to mines, and
the balanace to engine trouble, fire, and other causes. Air
Chief Marshal Tedder understandably disapproved of the wasteful

attempts to hold outposts in the Dodecanese. He said:

> One would have thought that some of the bitter
> lessons of Crete would have been sufficiently
> fresh in the mind to have prevented a repetition,
> and yet in the sad story of Kos and Leros we had
> the familiar cries and justifiable cries for
> protection from enemy air attack, complaints of
> inadequate support from the air, and heavy
> casualties in all three Services, because we were
> compelled once again to attempt the impossible.(9)

It is relevant to suggest that, even with the use of Turkish
airfields, there was no guarantee that operations from these
bases would have been effective in defending the islands. There
was no radar system in operation, and the advanced bases would
have been difficult to hold in the face of GAF operations over
the Aegean, particularly since Middle East Command had
relatively few fighter planes at its disposal.
Although both the Chief of the Imperial General Staff, Sir
Alan Brooke, and the Chief of Air Staff, Sir Charles Portal, on
various occasions expressed grave doubts on the wisdom of
continuing these operations, the Chiefs of Staff as a Committee
were always in support, that is, there was individual dissention
but collective support. A War Office report concluded:

> It is very improbable whether operations in the
> Aegean caused the withdrawal of any enemy
> resources from Italy; they possibly had some
> effect in preventing the despatch to the theatre
> of certain reinforcements. This fact should not
> be overlooked in view of the critical battle which
> followed the landings in Salerno and the
> subsequent expansion of our bridgehead. The
> position in Italy was not really secure until
> about 20 September.(10)

It should be pointed out, however, that the movement of the
main elements of 234 Brigade to the Dodecanese commenced after
20 September. Thus, to the extent that the retention of German
resources in the Aegean had any bearing on the Italian campaign,
this occurred after Salerno was deemed secure. The Brandenburger
Parachute Regiment used against Leros on 12 November, emplaned in
the Rome sector. All other German units employed in the Aegean
came from Greece or Crete.
During the period October-November, operations in the Aegean
did have the effect of diverting GAF units that would
otherwise have made sorties over Italy. Nevertheless, given
the preponderance of Allied air power in the central
Mediterranean, the diversion of GAF units to the Aegean would
not significantly have altered the balance of Allied air

superiority in the central sector. Allied air deficiency lay in the Aegean. The Germans had no fewer than twelve bomber bases within easy striking distance of the Dodecanese. Major-General David Lloyd Owen, LRDG, writing after the War, said:

> I believe we made our first of many blunders in so impotently failing to assume control over Rhodes. The failure to get airfields on the island should have been the signal that those Aegean operations were doomed to disaster unless Turkey could be persuaded at once to come in on the side of the Allies.(11)

> Thus ended the ill-starred battle for Leros. It was never a worthwhile risk, and when it was clear that it could not be given adequate air support I do not (and never did) understand why we did not cut our losses and withdraw with as much decorum as possible. But we did not do this, and we suffered an unnecessary and humiliating defeat.(12)

From the German point of view, a contemporary report stated: "The fighting showed that England's sea power which is engaged throughout the World's seas, was not able successfully to defend important bases in the eastern Mediterranean from where it had planned to put increasing pressure militarily."(13)

There is no doubt that the Germans fully exploited the situation in the Dodecanese with a relatively small force, certainly no larger than that deployed by the British. Moreover, the Germans were willing to absorb significantly higher casualties than were the Allies.

When dealing with dictatorial power there is always a danger if one utters a dissenting voice. The German Chiefs of Staff and commanders found this to be the case with Hitler, and it is a matter of record that the British Chiefs faced a similar jeopardy when confronted with the wrath of Churchill. The ghosts of Wavell, Ritchie, and Auchinleck were hovering in the background. There were some who felt it more prudent not to "make waves."

A War Office report draws a number of conclusions that call into question British strategy in the Aegean:

> The actions of the CIC Middle East, appear to have been much more closely aligned to the general tenor of personal telegrams to General Wilson from the Prime Minister than to the general tenor of the discussions in the official conferences at Tunis and on the occasion of the first visit of the Foreign Secretary to Cairo."(14)

Quotations from these telegrams support this contention:

9 September: This is the time to play high.
               Improvise and dare.

5 October: What are you going to do now to
               resist the attack on Leros and
               Samos to which you refer as
               likely?

9 October: You should press most strongly at
               the conference for further support
               for ACCOLADE, demand what is
               necessary and consult with
               Alexander. I am doing all I can.

14 October: My thoughts dwell constantly on
               Leros and generally this foothold
               in the Aegean. It would be a
               great triumph if you could keep it
               safely. I was very pleased with
               the way you used such poor bits
               and pieces as were left to you.
               Nil desperandum.(15)

On his return from Moscow on 5 November, the British Foreign
Secretary, Anthony Eden, reported from Cairo: "I feel happier
about Leros than when I was last here."(16) Within a week the
island was attacked, and after five days it fell. Should
politicians, even though members of the War Cabinet, be
entrusted with the responsibility of making purely military
decisions?

This account of British operations in the Aegean is drawn, in
the main, from an analysis of official reports. Was the
operation in support of Turkey (HARDIHOOD), a "phantom force",
or did it really exist? There is certainly nothing in the order
of the battle to indicate that an establishment was ever created.
What does emerge, time after time, is the unceasing effort on the
part of the Prime Minister to put together an assault force for
Rhodes, first from the Middle East and then, increasingly, from
the central Mediterranean, with the ultimate intent of bringing
Turkey into the War.

It is evident that these British inspired plans failed at every
turn because there was never any Allied agreement to mount major
operations in the Aegean or in the Balkans. The fact that
Churchill was willing to pour irreplaceable naval flotillas and
materiel in support of his Turkish chimera leads one to believe
that he truly was trying to expiate for the Dardanelles.
Churchill became obsessed with the Dodecanese. Certainly, the
pressure he brought to bear on President Roosevelt and General
Eisenhower suggests something more than a covert operation of
deception.

Winston Churchill has gone down in history as the man of the hour. He was a symbol. There are few who would disagree that his personality personified the bulldog spirit that, in the dark days of 1940, Britain so desperately needed. Few would disagree that his spirited leadership and his inspired personal relationship with President Roosevelt helped the West to buy time while the United States Government prepared itself and the American people to turn the tide. Nor does it deprecate Churchill's contribution to the War to make mention of the heroic sacrifices of Britain's fighter pilots, the untold agony of Russia, and the impact of Pearl Harbor on American attitudes. However, the Prime Minister's closest confidant, General Sir Alan Brooke said:

> His expectations outran what was achievable and caused him to seek what in the circumstances of the time was impossible. Planned strategy was not his strong card. He preferred to work by intuition and by impulses. He was never good at looking at all the implications of any course he favored. In fact, he frequently refused to look at them.(17)

The Prime Minister was a catalyst; he stimulated the British as no other man could do. He can be forgiven his failures. But it would be wrong to attribute the disaster in the Dodecanese to anybody other than Winston Churchill. It was he who sustained the effort; yet, in the last analysis could claim not even a pyrrhic victory. Ultimately, the Allies did not get bogged down in the Balkans, and for this we have the Americans to thank.

Brigadier Guy Prendergast, LRDG, wrote the following wry comment:

> I had just before the battle, been promoted Colonel, Raiding Forces, Aegean, which meant nothing since there was no raiding to be done just then. Jake Easonsmith, who was later killed on Leros, took over the unit and I was left in a rather thumb twiddling situation, doing odd jobs for Tilney.
>
> I would say, if asked, that the planners in HQME who I suppose were ordered to mount the operation by Churchill, should have firmly resisted doing so, unless fighter cover by the RAF was guaranteed. As you were there you will know the constant bombing by Stukas was a morale-sapping weapon. Churchill is reputed to have said that, for the purpose of this operation, cruisers must be considered as expendable, and they certainly were, mostly by bombing.

> Tilney took over, shortly before the invasion from
> a nitwit. I was very sorry for him as he never
> had the chance of getting the defenses in good
> order. The Germans were most efficient and with
> complete air superiority could have gone on
> reinforcing until we had to pack it in. A very
> sorry affair.(18)

The piecemeal lodgment of 234 Infantry Brigade, dispersed among three islands resulted in the brigade being decimated and the balance thrown into captivity. Losses to the Royal Navy included 32 ships and 750 officers and men. The RAF and USAAF had flown 3,746 sorties and lost 113 aircraft. These were the small costs which subsequently had to be borne. Rhodes remained in enemy hands.

Allied strategy in the Mediterranean was opportunistic, from Roosevelt's sanction for the TORCH landings to the subsequent assaults on Sicily and the Italian Peninsula. In the summer of 1943, the Balkans was a hot issue between Allied leaders and it has generated a great deal of argument ever since. The central figure in this controversy was Winston Churchill. Repeatedly he said: "I have never wished to send an army into the Balkans, but only by agents, supplies and commandos to stimulate the intense guerrilla [sic] prevailing there."(19)

Notwithstanding his disclaimer, one perceives that he had in mind the opening of a new front. The notion of a "third front" dealt with the question of the further use of Allied troops in the Mediterranean. One possibility was to move into southern France (ANVIL); another was to place under Allied threat the Adriatic coast in support of the Yugoslavs; a third was to secure the Aegean islands as a prerequisite to bringing Turkey into the War.

Churchill saw further opportunities in the eastern Mediterranean which in his mind should have taken precedence over a cross-Channel invasion. Initially he did not believe that the twenty-seven Anglo-American divisions (later increased to thirty-nine) were enough to assault the coast of France, and he also felt more was to be gained politically in bringing about the disintegration of German forces in Yugoslavia and Greece. In short, there was more to be achieved in the Mediterranean by establishing a bridgehead on the Dalmatian coast.

The British Prime Minister appears to have taken so many positions on the Balkans with Roosevelt, Stalin, and the Allied staffs that it is difficult to establish precisely what his real intentions were on this issue. AJP Taylor says:

> The policy of forestalling Russia in the Balkans
> was an invention of the postwar years. Romanian
> oil supplies were about exhausted. The Balkan
> countries, strictly speaking--Yugoslavia and

>Bulgaria--were pure burdens. Churchill's att-
>empted insistence on the Mediterranean did not
>spring from any desire to forestall Russia in the
>Balkans."(20)

Even so, the record is replete with attempts by the British
Prime Minister to bring Turkey into the War and for the Turks then
to attack Bulgaria. Michael Howard observes: "Rhodes and Rome
figured in his mind as necessary objectives . . . he wanted to
have his cake and eat it and his military advisors found
difficulty in convincing him that this was logistically
impossible."(21)

All that can be said with certainty is that Churchill did,
indeed, sponsor a massive military aid program for Turkey; he
sought to bring forty-six Turkish divisions into the conflict;
and he committed virtually the entire British Mediterranean fleet
in support of the British takeover of islands in the Dodecanese.

In his classic history of the Second World War, the Prime
Minister acknowledges the Aegean naval effort in these terms:
"The Royal Navy lent a helping hand."(22) This was, perhaps, his
only understatement of the entire war.

NOTES

1. CJC Molony et al., The Mediterranean and Middle East,
vol. 5, History of the Second World War (London: Her Majesty's
Stationery Office, 1973), 543.

2. Public Record Office, London, WO 106/3144.

3. Ibid.

4. Public Record Office, London, PREM 3/3/5.

5. AJP Taylor, English History, 1914-1945 (Oxford: Oxford
University Press, 1965), 572.

6. WO 106/3144.

7. Ibid.

8. Barrie Pitt, Special Boat Squadron: The Story of the
SBS in the Mediterranean (London: Century Publishing, 1983), 115.

9. Peter Smith and Edwin Walker, War in the Aegean
(London: William Kimber, 1974), 276.

10. WO 106/3144.

11. David Lloyd Owen, Providence Their Guide (London:
Harrap, 1980), 131.

12.   Ibid., 144.

13.   Das Signal, January 1944.

14.   WO 106/3144.

15.   Ibid.

16.   WO 106/3154.

17.   Sir Arthur Bryant, Triumph in the West (New York: Doubleday, 1957), 13.

18.   Brigadier GL Prendergast, Letter to the author, 6 October 1985.

19.   John Erhman, Grand Strategy, vol. 5, History of the Second World War (London: Her Majesty's Stationery Office, 1956), 95.

20.   AJP Taylor, English History, 1914-1945, 577.

21.   Michael Howard, The Mediterranean Strategy in the Second World War (New York: Frederick A. Praeger, Inc., 1968), 51.

22.   Winston S. Churchill, Closing the Ring (Boston: Houghton, Mifflin, 1951), 204.

Press Reports 1943

The Battles for Kos and Leros were fully reported in the British press over the period 16-21 November 1943. The most poignant account was written by L. Marsland Gander, The Daily Telegraph Special Correspondent and the only representative of the World press in the islands. On 19 November 1943, he reported: "The loss of Leros has taught us a bitter lesson. It is a disaster as big as Dieppe."(1)

The Spectator observed:

> The deplorable abandonment of Leros, following on the deplorable abandonment of Kos are reminders of the hard fact that there is no question of this war wearing itself away to its close. It will have to be fought to a close, and fought hard, fought as the Russians have been fighting it for months and years.
>
> Public opinion will not be satisfied until the whole question of Kos, Leros and Samos has been cleared up. What the public will want to know is who planned the expeditions against islands which could not be effectively reinforced by sea or protected from the air?
>
> Under whose direction were the forces on Leros and Samos kept in their hopeless position after Kos had proved a failure and the air support it might have rendered not forthcoming? And it must be asked, from whom in Whitehall emanates the lame and preposterous argument that the effect of the diversion of German effort needed to recapture Leros may prove equal to that caused by our fight for Greece and Crete?

The recent ill-judged expeditions to the Aegean
were undertaken when we have overwhelming superiority in the Mediterranean and when adventures
of this kind should be undertaken in sufficient
force or not at all. To adopt this course was to
make a present to the enemy of gallant troops and
the prestige of a local victory.(2)

Reynolds News reported:

The loss of Leros and the threat to Samos, following the loss of Kos is a distinct setback to
British prestige. It is a distinct and clear
announcement to the world that the German Army is
not beaten. The men of the German Army are still
fighting fiercely and their High Command in all
theatres is still displaying resolute determination not to yield an inch.

In the case of these islands the Germans will
regain some lost prestige in Turkey, a point
which should not have been overlooked in deciding
on our power to occupy and hold the islands.
This point is of sufficient importance for Mr.
Churchill in his last speech in the House, to
have said that: "A disastrous repulse at this
stage would be particularly vexatious."

If our occupation of Kos, Leros, and Samos had
really drawn heavily on German resources, there is
much to be said for them. But it is not at all
certain that they did. The occupation of these
islands did not really divert a single German
division. But it offered the enemy an opportunity
to strike at our unsupported detachments and
gobble them up.(3)

The Sunday Despatch Military Analyst wrote:

Our loss of Kos and Leros, key islands in the
eastern Mediterranean brings Allied higher
strategy under anxious survey. What happened?
On 16 September, the Allies attacked and captured
the islands from the Axis. A fortnight before, on
3 September, the Armistice conditions with Italy
had been signed. They were announced publicly on
8 September. And so it will be seen that our
responsible CIC in the Mediterranean took 13 days
to make up his mind to mount an attack against
islands of the highest strategical importance.

What was the effect of our attacks on Leros and the other islands on 16 September? We endangered the eastern flank of the entire German southern Balkan theatre of operations. We showed Turkey that we could safeguard her from any Aegean-borne German attack should Turkey be willing to cooperate by giving us bases. We gave a signal to Greek guerrillas inside the Peloponnese who were causing great trouble to the Axis occupying forces.(4)

These excerpts from the contemporary press are generally cogent and to the point. Written as they were, spontaneously and without the benefit of hindsight, they point to the twin problems of poor planning and equally poor execution resulting in the sacrifice of an entire infantry brigade, corps troops, and special forces. The press at the time did not have access to information on our naval losses which, as mentioned elsewhere in this book, were frightful; all to no avail because our reach exceeded our grasp. Indeed, who in Whitehall was responsible?

The military engagement of British troops on Kos and Leros was on a relatively small scale in terms of World War II operations. On the other hand, the naval force committed to the Aegean was, indeed, massive. British naval losses incurred in sustaining three small islands in the Dodecanese over a period of two months produced a very heavy toll among Royal Navy ships, due largely to enemy air attack. The effort sustained did not achieve the primary objectives (Rhodes and Turkey), nor the secondary objectives (Kos and Leros) which could not be held, no matter how great the naval sacrifice.

Apart from the official naval history, only one comprehensive account of this naval and military action has been published: War in the Aegean.(5) For the most part, a cloak of secrecy shrouds the strategy, planning, and execution of British operations in the Aegean. In his most recent book, The Korean War, Max Hastings has written: "In the cold accountancy of war and history there may be headlines to be extracted from defeat, but there is no virtue."(6)

NOTES

1. The Daily Telegraph, 19 November 1943. See also L. Marsland Gander, The Long Road to Leros (London: MacDonald, 1945.)

2. The Spectator, 19 November 1943.

3. Reynolds News, 21 November 1943.

4. The Sunday Despatch, 21 November 1943.

5.   Peter Smith and Edwin Walker, <u>War in the Aegean</u>. (London: William Kimber, 1974).

6.   Max Hastings, <u>The Korean War</u> (New York: Simon & Schuster, 1987), 226.

The author (far right) with two friends early in their military careers, on Malta, 1941.

Mediterranean Commanders. Back row, left to right: Air Chief Marshal Tedder, Admiral John Cunningham, General Alexander, General Bedell Smith. Front row, left to right: General Eisenhower, Mr. Churchill, General Wilson. By permission of The Trustees of The Imperial War Museum, London.

Italian coastal battery, Mount Clidi, covering Parteni and Blefuti Bays. Note exposed position—no casemates or camouflage.

Brandenburg paras in Athens preparing for Operation Leopard, the attack on Leros.

German assault on Leros, 12 November 1943. Paratroops cut the island in two between Gurna and Alinda Bays. Commandos carry out scramble landings at three key points.

2 a.m. Despatch

BATTLE OF LEROS DAY BY DAY

EYE-WITNESS ACCOUNT OF INVASION

BRITISH BRIGADIER LED DEFENCE OF H.Q.

A dramatic and connected account of the operations in Leros is given in the following despatch, received in London at 2 a.m. to-day, from L. Marsland Gander, Daily Telegraph war reporter and sole war correspondent on the island. An earlier despatch describing how Gander was taken off in a British destroyer two days before the garrison succumbed to overwhelming air attack is on P6.

From L. MARSLAND GANDER,
Daily Telegraph Special Correspondent, and the only representative of the world Press on the island

EASTERN MEDITERRANEAN BASE, Thursday.

The loss of Leros has taught a bitter lesson in air power. Though Leros had become practically an isolated strong-point behind the enemy lines, the decision to try to hold it was taken because of its strong natural defences.

It is a rocky switchback only 7½ miles long and at the narrowest point barely three-quarters of a mile wide. This wasp waist, roughly in the centre of the island, separates the two anchorages of Alinda and Burna Bays.

Farther south, the fine harbour of Portolago Bay bites deep into the island, leaving another narrow neck of land only half a mile wide. The dangerous supply routes to Leros, hundreds of miles long, passed close to enemy airfields and were harried continually by the Luftwaffe.

Our ships had their best chance of slipping through at night, but had to endeavour to be under our own fighter umbrella by daylight. Despite all the difficulties, we had, however, managed to land British troops of famous regiments in the island. These were additional to an Italian garrison, consisting of several thousand marines, soldiers and sailors.

Only about 2,000 of the Italians were first-line fighters, the remainder being technical and line of communication men. All the heights dominating the three main bays were commanded by Italian batteries, generally of 90 mm. guns.

WARSHIPS AS TRANSPORTS

We had made determined efforts, chiefly by using H.M. warships as transports, to strengthen the anti-aircraft defences, but up to the time of invasion had only succeeded in landing some Bofors and a few heavier guns.

The garrison was, however, well equipped with automatic arms of all kinds, and the main defensive position, Mount Meraviglia, 600 feet high, was studded with machine-gun nests.

My conducting officer and I, after a journey which owing to various misadventures, had lasted a week and had involved our travelling in eight different vessels, landed from a motor-launch in Alinda Bay on the night of Nov. 11.

The movement control officer who courteously greeted us at the jetty remarked as we piled into a jeep that there was another " flap " on, but as that was the usual form in Leros no one showed any great concern.

We made our way to " B " mess, a house beside the bay, on the outskirts of Leros town. The town, I gathered, was completely deserted.

Many of the Greek inhabitants had fled the island in caiques, and others has taken refuge in caves.

In six weeks, Leros had had a thousand enemy air sorties, but the damage had not been remarkable and the number of casualties was very small indeed. Only two persons had been killed.

We lay down to sleep on trestle beds but, night-long, the roar of aircraft overhead and spasmodic A.A. fire kept us awake.

There had been heavy bombing raids all that day, but at night, according to their habit, the Stukas and Jus stayed at home. Though aircraft passed over continuously there was no bombing and the object of the demonstration was not clear.

" ACTION STATIONS "

At 4 a.m. an orderly stumbled up the dark stairway to report in a quiet matter-of-fact voice that a motor-launch had sighted an invasion fleet. We were to proceed to action stations.

I grabbed a tin hat, a trench coat, my typewriter, and a few other essentials and, with my conducting captain, followed the other officers down the road.

At the transit camp a few hundred yards away we found a jeep loading up, and we leaped on the bonnet for a lift up to battle headquarters on Mount Meraviglia. These were in a tunnel blasted through the mountain peak with two main chambers opening off.

One entrance where there was a Bren gun nest, gave a magnificent view over the Alinda and Gurna Bays. Below was Leros town which, in the early morning light, looked as if it had been built with a child's box of coloured bricks.

Brigadier Robert Tilney and Generalleutnant Frederic Müller congenially reflect on the outcome of the battle for Leros.

Stalag VIIA, Mosburg, Germany, home for many of the 234 Infantry Brigade after fifteen days and nights in a prison train, by permission of The Trustees of the Imperial War Museum, London.

Part II
Operational Perspectives

Air Forces in the Aegean

There was always an air threat from the GAF, and invariably it materialized. The British allocated 280 aircraft to the Aegean, based on Cyprus and on Kos. These were later reinforced by USAAF and RAF Northwest African Command aircraft which flew 3,746 sorties in support of operations in the Aegean. The British Beaufighter, no match for the Luftwaffe Fw 190s or Me 109s, suffered 50 percent losses among its squadrons. The two key problems for the British were the lack of air bases to facilitate the operation and the lack of short range fighter aircraft.

The other related problem was the need to maintain a bomber force to neutralize the German air bases in Greece, on Rhodes, and on Crete. This could only be done intermittently, by US ninth Bomber Command and two RAF heavy bomber squadrons; the former under command of Mediterranean Air Command (MAC), and the latter under HQME.

Mediterranean Air Command was very concerned about the way in which the Aegean operations had developed, involving ACM Tedder in commitments that he had no prior way of assessing. Moreover, the diversion of air forces in the Aegean directly affected Allied operations in the Italian theatre. ACM Tedder considered that the procedure by which General Wilson launched operations without full consultation with General Eisenhower and AFHQ was most dangerous.

Among the islands occupied by the British only Kos had an airfield; it was, therefore, the primary target for the GAF. On 13 September, two Ju 88 reconnaissance aircraft were destroyed. On 17 September, ten enemy vessels escorted by a destroyer were shadowed by Baltimores of 201 Group until they were attacked by a strike of eight Beaufighters of 237 Wing operating from Limmassol. Two Beaufighters were severely damaged by flak; one crash-landed at its base, killing the navigator, while the other returned safely on one engine. On the same day a Ju 52 was shot down by a Spitfire operating from Kos.

The long awaited discovery by the enemy of the RAF presence

at Antimachia airfield on Kos led to two attacks on the 18 September. The first was made by a single Ju 88, the second by seven Ju 88s escorted by five Me 109s. Two Spitfires were lost and three Dakotas hit the water when flying low to avoid interception. The GAF lost five Ju 88s and one Me 109. Two Beaufighters flew intruder patrols over Crete; one was hit and crash-landed.

The next day, Antimachia was again attacked by five Ju 88s and ten Me 109s which carried out lowlevel bombing and strafing. One Spitfire was destroyed, and two Dakotas were burned on the ground. The enemy lost one Me 109. On the same day, seven Beaufighters of 237 Wing were on an offensive sweep north of Rhodes and made no sightings. Six Hurricanes of 213 Squadron swept the sea on a broad front between Cyprus and Kastellorizo, while at night two Beaufighters of thirty-ninth Squadron intruded onto Crete.

At dawn on the 20 September, another attack was made on Antimachia by two He 111 dropping butterfly bombs and ground strafing. One Heinkel was shot down by a Beaufighter and the second raider was destroyed by the AA defenses. A second raid was made later in the morning by three Ju 88s and four Me 109s.

During the period leading up to the enemy assault on Kos, efforts were made to open up new landings strips. This work had to be done by pick and shovel in the absence of airfield engineering machinery such as tractors and bulldozers. With these limited resources, an airstrip 1,150 yards long was constructed. This strip enabled Dakotas to resume their ferrying of supplies. At midday on the 20 September, six Spitfires were able to land, and a bomb disposal unit was flown in by Beaufighters.

On 26 September, the GAF attacked HMS INTREPID and HHMS QUEEN OLGA in Portolago Harbor on Leros. A second attack was made by two formations of Ju 88s. Both destroyers were sunk. Spitfires from Kos engaged the enemy force, and one Ju 88 was destroyed. The next day, twenty Ju 88s attacked Antimachia escorted by Me 109s. One Spitfire was damaged on the ground and two were missing; no enemy losses were reported. During the afternoon another attack was made by a strong force of Ju 88s and Me 109s. The enemy was engaged by Spitfires on patrol; one Me 109 and two Cant Z 501 were destroyed for the loss of one Spitfire. Antimachia airfield was rendered unserviceable and there were more casualties on the ground.

Kos was again attacked on 28 September, by twenty-four low flying Ju 88s escorted by Me 109s. No fighter defense could be taken as both airfields were out of commission. A second attack was made that day against the Kos landing ground by fifteen Ju 88s, again escorted by Me 109s. Two sections of Spitfires intercepted, forcing part of the enemy formation to jettison their bombs. Two Spitfires were missing. During the day, nine Spitfires of seventy-fourth Squadron left Nicosia to reinforce 234 Wing on Kos. Eight arrived over Kos in time to participate in the second attack.

On the 29 September, eighteen Ju 88s escorted by twelve Me 109s raided Antimachia. Seventeen craters were made and thirteen unexploded bombs fell on the landing ground. Two sections of Spitfires intercepted and one Ju 88 was destroyed. After this raid, the Spitfires had to operate from a third strip that had been constructed. That afternoon, twenty-four Ju 88s escorted by Me 109s again attacked Antimachia. Forty craters were made on the runway and a number of delayed action bombs were dropped. The RAF signal station was damaged and again there were some casualties.

The new landing strip near the town of Kos had been used by Dakotas each night, and every effort was made to conceal this procedure from the enemy. But at dawn on 28 September, an enemy reconnaissance discovered the presence of a Dakota which had been unable to leave the night before, although it had been towed off the runway and every effort made to conceal it by camouflage. The subsequent attack destroyed this landing ground, and from then on all supplies had to be dropped by parachute. Antimachia was bombed again on the following day and was rendered useless. Moreover, the 1,150 yard landing strip that had been constructed on the saltpans between Antimachia and Kos was found to be flooded by a blocked drain.

By this time the defense system was chaotic. No transport or telephonic communications were available until the evening of the 2 October. Meanwhile, the infantry withdrew to the wadis and other suitable cover until the airfield could be brought into use again and fresh plans made. In the town of Kos, the troops were scattered in cottages and schools and were without transport. No ground defenses were dug or posts prepared. The prevalent impression was that the troops were about to be moved.(1)

On 3 October, the situation on Kos was critical. Middle East Command asked AFHQ for six squadrons of Lightnings or Mustangs to cover movement of naval craft by day in the Dodecanese. MEHQ also requested that the transport group promised for ACCOLADE be despatched to them at once and that MAC's bombing program should be extended to cover airfields on Crete and Rhodes. The Prime Minister sent a message to Air Chief Marshal Tedder: "Kos is highly important and a reverse there would be most vexatious."(2) As a result, two groups of Liberators were sent to Benghazi to operate for two days. Four groups of Fortresses were to attack Greek airfields on 4 October, while Mitchells and Lightnings were directed upon the same targets. Meanwhile, Kos had fallen into German hands.

MEHQ informed Mediterranean Air Command that they attached great importance to a continuation of sustained attacks on the Greek airfields in order to reduce the effectiveness of the GAF in the Aegean. Their aim was to prevent the enemy from reinforcing Rhodes, to prevent attacks on Leros, Samos, or Symi by dispersing enemy shipping concentrations, to improve information about Kos, Kalymnos, and Stampalia, and to help build up Kastellorizo as a secure advanced base. All these reactive demands were made a month after Wilson had embarked on the Aegean venture, and only after the fall of Kos.

General Eisenhower was sympathetic and wrote to Tedder, but he cautioned that he could not forget the mission given to the Italian theatre by the Combined Chiefs of Staff and could not disperse strength from the central Mediterranean. In view of the diminishing power of the Lightnings due to the temporary suspension of replacements, Eisenhower had to conserve these groups. As a consequence, no firm commitments could be made to help Middle East Command.

The matter of assisting General Wilson had not been referred to Eisenhower by the Combined Chiefs of Staff: "It had been handled on the basis of cooperation and upon suggestions from London."(3) General Eisenhower could not, however, jeopardize the campaign in Italy. The Allied Commander felt that if ACCOLADE depended upon a firm commitment for the diversion of air force groups from the central Mediterranean then ACCOLADE would have to be postponed.

ACM Tedder was prepared to send six Mitchell Bomber Groups armed with 75mm cannon for air attacks on Leros convoy concentrations. In fact, only twelve Mitchells and six air transport aircraft were sent to Gambut, and these were told to remain long enough to make two sorties. The MAC promised to go on bombing the Greek airfields. Later it was decided to leave the Mitchells in the Middle East, subject to recall to MAC at twenty-four hours notice.

On 26 October, Middle East Command asked for bombing attacks on Greek airfields to be intensified. Tedder felt that a move of two groups of ninth (US) Bomber Command back to Benghazi would be unwise; they could not then operate against more northerly targets. Also, they could not then be operated as part of the heavy bomber force and their operational capacity would become circumscribed by distance and bad weather. He felt, "that the Aegean situation did not require the full use of these groups in addition to the forces already available in the Middle East."(4)

Of the three groups of long-range fighters available, one was employed against Middle East targets although it was also working with the Mitchells in the heel of Italy. Tedder felt that the Mitchells must have P-38 escort if they were to operate effectively. In any case, the Lightnings were achieving better results than the bombers in hitting enemy aircraft dispersed on various landing fields.

The release to the Aegean of two squadrons of Lightning groups would have affected the operation of the whole of the strategic air force. Tedder and Eisenhower were firmly opposed to such transference and resisted any movement that would result in the air force being placed in a position where it could not take on strategic targets in northern Italy, France, or Austria.

During October, aircraft under Mediterranean Air Command had flown 1,500 sorties against targets in the Balkans, the majority against planes on the ground. All this was in addition to what had been done by forces operating directly under Middle East Command. Despite this, Tedder was continually being subjected to pressure to revise the decisions of the La Marsa meeting and divert further air forces to the Middle East. The ACM had a feeling that, "the old [and he hoped discredited] process of building up the air as an alibi for failure was once again in full swing."(5)

Tedder could not say how far failure to hold Kos was or was not due to weakness in planning or execution, but to him it was clear that once Kos had fallen and effective air cover no longer possible, one of the main foundations of all Aegean operations had collapsed. Tedder said, "I feel this false alibi needs smashing whenever it rears its ugly head and have told Douglas so."(6) ACM Sir William Sholto Douglas, AOC in C Middle East, drew the logical deduction from the loss of the fighter bases at Kos: that HQME should evacuate Leros and Samos. The only solution following the fall of Kos was to evacuate the garrisons on these two islands.

During the second half of October, the Luftwaffe switched its attack to Leros. The first phase was designed to neutralize the island's defenses. Dive-bombers from Stukageschwader 87 operating from Rhodes and HI III's flying from more distant airfields on the Greek mainland attacked Portolago AA gun emplacements, and infantry defensive positions. During the first phase, the Luftwaffe flew more than 1,000 sorties against Leros but the island's AA Bofors guns, few in number, had not been knocked out.

Throughout the five-day action, the GAF supported their troops with 145 planes, tactical bombers (Ju 88s), and dive-bombers (Ju 87s). The dive-bombers continually attacked the British positions throughout the daylight hours. There were never fewer than ten Stukas circling overhead. The Germans used their dive-bombers as artillery, for observation, and for close support. On occasion, the Stukas bombed close to the exposed positions of the German paras and caused heavy casualties among their own troops.

In October, against Leros, the GAF mounted 140 attacks employing a total of 1,200 aircraft. This assault intensified during the first two weeks of November, culminating in the destruction of the British garrison. Dominance in the air was the key factor in determining the outcome of the battles for both Kos and Leros. By 1 October, GAF strength in the Aegean area had increased to 285 operational aircraft and seventy-seven transport aircraft. These numbers included, fifty-four fighters, sixty-eight long-range bombers and sixty-nine dive-bombers.

The Luftwaffe had cooperated with Leutenantgeneral Mueller's troops in an exemplary fashion. The Germans had achieved local air superiority before and during the action on Kos, and total dominance of the air over Leros. The GAF sank or crippled four British cruisers, five destroyers, five minesweepers, and coastal craft.

Allied air support for naval and military operations in the Aegean amounted to 3,746 sorties by bombers of the US ninth Bomber Command, USAAF Lightnings, RAF Spitfires, and Beaufighters. Lost aircraft numbered 113, and more than 355 aircrew personnel were killed in these operations.

Demonstrably, single-engine fighter planes could not operate for long from advanced bases in the Aegean. In fact, the British did not have such bases. Nor was it possible to operate from Turkish airfields and, in any event, none were made available. It is also true that, even if the task force had been able to hold Kos as a base for Spitfire operations to cover Leros and Samos, this was, indeed, a slender thread. It would not have offset the GAF capability one iota. The Germans operated from twelve bomber bases located in the eastern Mediterranean, identified as follows:

Greece	Crete	Rhodes
Eleusis	Heraklion	Calato
Kalamaki	Kastelli-Pediada	Maritza
Tatoi	Tymbaki	Cattavia
Sedes	Maleme	
Larissa		

Once the Spitfire umbrella over Kos had been destroyed, there was never any attempt to provide the Leros garrison with close air support; there were no planes and there were no airfields. Allied bombing of Greek airfields was never enough to interdict all the bomber bases available to the GAF in the eastern Mediterranean.

NOTES

1. Public Record Office, London, WO 106/3149.

2. Public Record Office, London, AIR 41/53.

3. Public Record Office, London, PREM 3/3/5.

4. AIR 41/53.

5. Ibid.

6. Ibid.

Lockheed *P-38 Lightnings* essential to the war operations in the Aegean, Smithsonian Institution Photo No. 29227/40806 A. C., by permission of the Smithsonian Institution.

HMS Pathfinder, closed down for battle stations and moving at high speed, courtesy of Captain C. W. Malins, RN.

Naval Operations
in the Aegean

The center of operations lay 350 miles from the main British naval base at Alexandria, a distance that created difficulties in fueling destroyers and restrictions on fighter protection, which had to be flown from Egypt, Cyrenaica, or Cyprus. Operations for Hunt Class destroyers were limited to two nights in the Aegean before they had to refuel.

Because of the vulnerability of the Dodecanese Islands to air attack by the GAF, it was decided that British ships should proceed to the Turkish coast to lie up during daylight hours. The Turks accommodated British ships taking refuge in their territorial waters. Even Hitler respected this bending of Turkey's neutrality inasmuch as he refused to permit Luftwaffe formations to bomb British ships while lying off the Turkish coast.

The comparative strengths of Naval forces in the Aegean on 8 September were as follows:

Allied:

Fleet destroyers	6
Hunt Class destroyers	2
First Submarine Flotilla	10
(with additions from tenth SF)	
ML	16
LSF (Levant Schooner Flotilla caiques)	10
RAF High Speed Launches	3
Total	47

Opposing enemy naval forces:

Destroyers (ex Italian Navy)	5
E-Boats	4
R-Boats	6

Opposing enemy naval forces:

Escort Vessels	6
Total	21

Plus a number of auxiliaries, Siebal ferries, F-Boats, I-Boats (60ft Assault Craft), and Armed Tugs

From the outset, the role of the Royal Navy was to support isolated land bases. "The Navy's task was two-fold, to build-up British forces and supplies on the islands, and to intercept German shipping between Piraeus and the Dodecanese."(1)

On 10 September, two MLs arrived in Kastellorizo from Cyprus with a small party of garrison troops, civil affairs officer, and sixty members of the SBS. The party at Kastellorizo was joined on 13 September by B Company 2 RWK, who remained on the island for two weeks, plus 300 troops and stores destined for Kos and Leros. The troops were carried on four ships, the Free French La MAQUEUSE and COMMANDANT DOMAINE, the Indian ship HMIS SUTLEJ, and the Greek ship HHMS KONDOURIOTIS. By 14 September, missions had been established on Kos, Leros, and Samos. Three hundred officers and men of the 2 RIF arrived on Leros on 17 September in HMS HURWORTH and CROOME.

On 18 September, HMS FAULKNOR and ECLIPSE with HHMS QUEEN OLGA sank two merchant ships (3,000 and 1,200 tons) north of Stampalia. On 23 September, HMS ECLIPSE sank a 2,500-ton Italian merchant ship (SS DENIZETTI) off the southwest point of Rhodes after it had landed German reinforcements on the island and was returning westward with Italian prisoners-of-war.

Meanwhile, the enemy was sending raiding forces to the Cyclades to evacuate the Italian garrisons and to seize war materiel and supplies. During this time, a Greek submarine, HHMS/M KATSONIS on patrol in the Gulf of Athens, was destroyed by enemy anti-submarine craft. Within two weeks of the initial excursion by the British into the Dodecanese, operations entered a new phase which was the start of the German offensive. On 26 September, HMS INTREPID and HHMS QUEEN OLGA were attacked by eight Ju 88s in the harbor at Portolago, Leros.

There was no warning, and no Italian AA guns opened fire, but INTREPID shot down one of the attacking aircraft. INTREPID was damaged, and the QUEEN OLGA was hit aft and sank. This attack certainly demonstrated the inefficiency of the AA defenses on Leros. The Italian plotters, predictors, and AA fire defense plan were not set up to deal with lowflying aircraft. On 26 September, 40mm Bofors guns had yet to be installed on the island.

On 1 October, the Italian destroyer EURO, lying in Partheric Bay, was attacked by twenty-two Ju 88s and went aground. By this time, the naval forces of Hunt Class destroyers had been increased to nineteen (including five Greek and one Polish).

Their range was limited, and they could not look for support from the fleet destroyers which, on 1 October, sailed from Alexandria to Malta as escorts for HMS HOWE and KING GEORGE V.

This temporary detachment of the fleet destroyers left the Hunts in a most vulnerable position. On the night of 2-3 October, due to fuel limitations, ALDENHAM, MIAOULIS, and THEMISTOCLES were unable to intercept an enemy convoy reported to be steering eastward from Naxos. From intelligence received it was believed that this convoy was bound for Rhodes, though in fact it was the invasion force that landed on Kos at 0500 hrs 3 October.

The German invasion force that assaulted Kos included seven transports, two destroyers, E-Boats and R-Boats, seven landing craft, and some caiques. Troops were landed, and paratroops were dropped in the center of the island. By nightfall, the enemy had 2,000 troops on Kos. Allied naval losses so far were KATSONIS, QUEEN OLGA, INTREPID, and the Italian destroyer EURO. From this point on, all British naval losses were incurred in an effort to sustain Leros alone.

The Admiralty immediately ordered naval reinforcements to the Aegean. The twelfth Cruiser squadron sailed from Malta. It comprised SIRIUS and DIDO with the anti-aircraft cruiser CARLISLE. Two fleet destroyers were also detailed from Taranto, bringing the total of Aegean Fleet destroyers to ten. From the night of 5-6 October, a force of cruisers and destroyers patrolled the Kaso and Scarpanto Straits.(2)

On the night of 6-7 October, a force of two cruisers and two destroyers (SIRIUS, PENELOPE, FAULKNOR, and FURY) entered the Aegean to intercept enemy reinforcements approaching the Dodecanese from the west. This force was assisted by an enemy report from HMS/M UNRULY and was able to locate and sink an enemy convoy consisting of an ammunition ship, an armed trawler, and six enemy landing craft. The sinking of this convoy delayed the enemy assault on Leros.

On 8 October, UNRULY torpedoed and sank an enemy minelayer south of Amorgos. As the SIRIUS force was leaving the Aegean through the Scarpanto Straits, a heavy air attack developed, and PENELOPE was hit by an unexploded bomb and suffered damage from four near misses. A squadron of P-38s were giving air cover, but had to withdraw as they jettisoned their longrange tanks for action.

Another sweep was made at night by a force of one cruiser (HMS CARLISLE) and four destroyers. Proceeding south through Scarpanto Straits, the force was heavily attacked by twenty-five Ju 87s and Ju 88s. Although the escorting Lightnings shot down no fewer than sixteen enemy aircraft, PANTHER was hit and sunk; and CARLISLE was hit aft and was towed to Alexandria by ROCKWOOD. On the 11 October, the Lightnings were withdrawn for service in the central Mediterranean.

Intelligence now indicated that the enemy would stage an invasion of Leros from Kos and Kalymnos with the 4,000 troops positioned on these two islands. At noon on 15 October, an enemy convoy of two merchant ships and two landing craft was reported eastbound off Naxos. Two destroyers, BELVOIR and BEAUFORT, left their hideout in Turkish waters to intercept and destroy it. They were heavily attacked by Ju 87s and 88s. The convoy was diverted northwards, and the destroyers then withdrew due to lack of fuel. One cruiser and two destroyers (PHOEBE, FAULKNOR, and FURY) continued the search through the night of 15-16 October.

The next day, HMS/M TORBAY sighted the same convoy north of Levitia and sank one of the merchant ships. The second ship was sunk by SIRIUS and PENN during their bombardment of Port Kalymnos after landing stores and personnel at Alinda Bay on Leros. On the night of 17-18 October, HURSLEY and MIAOULIS set a small merchant ship on fire, sank an E-Boat and a landing craft, and set fire to a sloop. Gunfire from his sloop slightly damaged the HURSLEY.

The losses to enemy shipping so far greatly reduced enemy chances of invading Leros for the time being. In the ensuing days, efforts could have been made either to evacuate the 1,000 man garrison on Leros or to reinforce it; the risk to British naval forces was no different. In any event, the decision had been made earlier to hold the island.

HMS HEDGEHOG from the Levant Schooner Flotilla had left Leros for Levitia to evacuate forty-eight German prisoners-of-war previously taken by the LRDG. Unfortunately, the flotilla had engine trouble on the return trip. The Germans seized control of the HEDGEHOG, which was found burning in the harbor. The re-occupation of Levitia, which is only fifteen miles west of Leros, was a pointer to the Germans' intention to attack Leros itself.

In the afternoon of the 17 October, two cruisers-AURORA and SIRIUS-and three destroyers, escorted by four Beaufighters were south of Scarpanto Straits when they were attacked by a strong formation of Ju 88s. The SIRIUS was hit aft (casualties: fourteen dead and thirty wounded) but its hull remained intact, and it was able to proceed to Alexandria. On the night of 18-19 October, the Kos roads and inner harbor were bombarded by BELVOIR, HURWORTH, and BEAUFORT at close range. HURWORTH was hit by shore batteries. PHOEBE fired 350 rounds into Port Kalymnos, and FURY marked the north shore of Kos; both ships were bombed but not hit.

The next night, FURY and BEAUFORT proceeded along the north coast of Kos, bombarding the Kos roads before proceeding southward to rendezvous with AURORA, which had bombarded the port of Rhodes with HHMS MIAOULIS. Air reconnaissance of Kalymnos revealed that a 150-foot naval auxiliary, a 300-foot M/V, and two F-Boats were in the area; four were operational, each designed to carry 200 to 300 troops.

On the night of 21-22 October, FAULKNOR, PETARD, and DULVERTON went on offensive patrol. They rendezvoused with AURORA and MIAOULIS and returned to Alexandria. Early on the morning of the 21 October, JERVIS, HURWORTH, PATHFINDER, and ADRIAS left

Alexandria for the Aegean. The fleet destroyers (JERVIS and PATHFINDER) had stores and troops for Leros but, owing to the time of moonrise, had to lieup in the Gulf of Kos on the 22nd.

The two Hunts, while proceeding to create a diversion south of Leros to cover the landing of stores by the fleets, ran into a newly laid minefield east of Kalymnos. The ADRIAS had its forecastle blown off and beached itself on a sandy bottom in Gumusluk Harbor. Twenty-one were killed and twenty-one were wounded. The HURWORTH was broken in two, and both parts sank in fifteen minutes. The total number of survivors was sixty-five and about one hundred of the crew drowned.

On 23 October, one cruiser and six destroyers (two fleets and four Hunts) left Alexandria for the Aegean. The fleets, ECLIPSE and PETARD, each carried 200 officers and men of the Fourth Battalion of The Buffs Regiment. At 0005hrs 24 October, while proceeding through the Karabakla Channel, ECLIPSE struck a mine and sank within minutes. Seven officers, 128 soldiers, and over 135 of the ship's company drowned. A total of 136 survivors (soldiers and sailors) were rescued.

Intelligence reports at this stage indicated that enemy ships in Piraeus were now ready to sail for Samos and that 4,000 German alpine troops were ready to embark. It was also reported that thirteen sixty-foot powered lighters of the I-Boat class had arrived in Athens by rail. Further intelligence reports attributed the enemy's failure to launch an attack on Leros to the continued presence of British ships and aircraft.

Photo reconnaissance of Kalamaki airfield on 28 October revealed eight Dornier bombers, which carried rocket bombs, and showed a new effort was to be launched against Allied ships. On 29 October, HMS/M UNSPARING, south of Amorgos, fired four torpedoes, sank an eastbound troopship of 1,200 tons, and later, with one torpedo, sank in the same position an R-Boat stopped and loaded with survivors. Meanwhile, the CIC Middle East decided to reinforce the Leros garrison bringing its strength up to 2,500.

On the afternoon of 30 October, AURORA and three destroyers escorted by Beaufighters were attacked by a formation of Ju 87s and 88s. The Beaufighter escorts shot down one Ju 88 in the first attack and four in the second. AURORA was hit by a bomb, which put all her four-inch guns out of action, killed forty-six, and wounding twenty. The AURORA then returned to Alexandria with BEAUFORT. The remaining destroyers, PETARD and BELVOIR, continued toward the Aegean and were again bombed. Both ships returned to Kastellorizo. On 2 November, HMS/M SIMOON was on patrol between Naxos and Mykonos; on the 5th it was diverted to a point five miles west of Tenedo. It was not heard from again and is presumed to have struck a mine and sunk with all hands.

The enemy possessed complete air superiority in the area and had shown every intention of attacking ships underway in Turkish waters. The German invasion fleet was expected to arrive at Kos and Kalymnos on the night of the 9th or early on 10 November.

Bombardment of these two places was carried out by PETARD and ROCKWOOD with the Polish destroyer KRAKOWIAK. Fifteen hundred rounds of four-inch shells were poured into Kalymnos. Another force of destroyers, FAULKNOR and BEAUFORT with HHMS PINDOS, bombarded Kos harbor. PETARD and ROCKWOOD were later attacked with glider bombs. ROCKWOOD was hit by an unexploded bomb in the gearing room and the compartment flooded.

Air reconnaissance showed considerable movement of landing craft between Kos and Kalymnos. The destroyer force lay up in the Gulf of Kos in order to conserve fuel. BEAUFORT and PINDOS were then ordered to attack landing craft on Kos. ML 456 on patrol to the east of Alinda Bay sighted and reported enemy forces twelve miles east of Leros proceeding north, and later re-engaged a force of two destroyers and ten landing craft. ML 456 was damaged and forced to return to Alinda Bay, where it landed wounded.

Three more destroyers, DULVERTON, ECHO, and BELVOIR, entered the Aegean late on 12 November. Picked up by enemy aircraft, they were shadowed and attacked with glider bombs in the Gulf of Kos. DULVERTON was hit and sunk; eighty-five were drowned. ECHO and BELVOIR picked up six officers and 103 ratings. ML 358 was hit by a shell off Leros and lost with all hands. During the night ECHO and BELVOIR bombarded enemy positions on Mount Appetici. Further destroyer reinforcements (PENN, ALDENHAM, and BLENCATHRA) entered the Aegean on the 13th.

British troop reinforcements, the 2 RWK, were embarked on the night 14-15 November from Samos by ECHO and BELVOIR. The ECHO, proceeding at thirty knots, managed to land 250 troops at Portolago before daylight on the 15th. But BELVOIR with its slower speed was forced to lie up off the Turkish coast in Pharlah Bay, where it transferred its 150 troops to MTBs and BYMs for passage to Leros later that evening.

Reinforcements from Samos were also landed at Portolago by MS 103 and two MLs. At dusk on 14 November, enemy positions in Alinda Bay were attacked from seaward by PENN, ALDENHAM, and BLENCATHRA. They attacked three enemy caiques and bombarded targets ashore. PENN and its force then patrolled the area being repeatedly attacked by enemy aircraft, including glider bombs. ECHO sank an F-Lighter and two landing barges, all laden with troops. ECHO and BELVOIR withdrew from the Aegean on the 16th.

By the morning of 15 November, British forces on Leros had been reinforced by about 400 troops, and the enemy was deprived of some of its reinforcements. Air reconnaissance reported assault craft southeastward of Kalymnos and steering northward, straight for Leros. Owing to W/T, delays this report was not received until midnight. There was still time for the PENN's force to have proceeded to intercept those craft, but PENN remained at anchor in the Gulf of Mandelyah and did not proceed till dawn, with the ALDENHAM, to carry out a sweep close east of Leros. However, the enemy reinforcements had already landed.

PENN was shelled and holed above the waterline. Both ships then withdrew-with eighty wounded transferred by small craft from Leros-bombarding Kos harbor on their way to join BLENCATHRA who was towing ROCKWOOD to Alexandria. Their place in the battle was taken by FURY, EXMOOR, and the Polish destroyer KRAKOWIAK. But it was the beginning of the end for the British troops.

The naval staff on Leros were at Battle HQ on Mount Meraviglia. When it appeared that they would be overrun, orders were given to destroy all naval signals publications. From then on, signaling with the SBNO had to be done through Army channels, using Army ciphers, which seriously interfered with communications and, therefore, operations. The last radio link with Leros went off the air at 1947hrs on 16 November. Landing of the Greek Sacred Squadron (from Samos) was canceled. Orders were then given to the Navy to evacuate any survivors and to withdraw the remaining force on Samos.

Plans to meet such an emergency had been made in mid-October. SBS patrols were landed on Leros to assist any British troops still at liberty, and an RAF launch and Levant schooner successfully evacuated LRDG troops from Seriphos and Mykoni. The evacuation of Samos was carried out by caiques under the direction of the Military Attache in Turkey. On the night of 27-28 November, the last British garrison from the Dodecanese battle area was withdrawn from Kastellorizo. HHMS ADRIAS-minus its bow-left the Turkish coast on 1 December and reached Alexandria under its own steam five days later.

So ended the Battle for Leros, which, though on a smaller scale, resembled the Gallipoli operations in 1915. The casualties incurred by the Royal Navy and the supporting Allied naval units in their attempts to sustain Leros were very severe. On successive nights, Allied cruisers and destroyers moved at high speed into the hazardous waters of the Aegean. There was an air of tense expectancy as the ships then proceeded slowly through mine-infested channels; disaster pending.

Laying up by day provided no respite. As Allied ships steamed to rendezvous points, they were attacked by dive-bombers, Ju 88s and Dornier glider bombs. Ships were hit by high explosive bombs with devastating effect while fires raged simultaneously in forward and aft sections of the ships. HMS SIRIUS was hit aft with fourteen killed and thirty wounded; PANTHER sunk with heavy loss of life; ADRIAS was mined and twenty-one were killed and twenty-one wounded; ECLIPSE was mined and 267 killed and fifty wounded; DULVERTON was glider bombed and eighty-five were killed; ML 388 was shelled and lost with all hands; AURORA was hit by a bomb, killing forty-six and wounding twenty; HURWORTH was mined and 100 were killed; SIMOON sank with all hands-and so the list goes on. All but four ships were lost or heavily damaged after the fall of Kos. A total of thirty-two ships were sunk or crippled with the loss of over 750 officers and ratings.

Meanwhile, night after night, the Royal Navy transported guns, jeeps, stores, and men to the islands, defending themselves against repeated aircraft attacks.   Intercepting and engaging convoys, bombarding shore targets, and evacuating wounded were ongoing tasks.   Bofors guns were broken down and strapped to the casing of Royal Navy submarines which then brought them to Leros. In narrow waters and near known or suspected minefields, prolonged patrols were maintained owing to local emergencies, which required that submarines and surface ships remain on station.

A summary of losses to RN and Allied ships (Table 12.1) gives some indication of the sacrifice made to sustain the action in the Aegean over a limited period of two months, 14 September-14 November, 1943.

Table 12.1

Nominal List of Allied Ships Lost in the Aegean

Ship	Sunk	Crippled	Captured
Cruiser		4	
Destroyer	6	4	
Submarines	3	4	
LCT	2		
LCM			1
MTB		1	
ML	4	1	
Schooner			1
BYMS			1
TOTAL:	15	14	3

Source: Admiralty, Official Naval History, ADM 234/364.

As noted, nearly one-half (46 percent) of British naval losses were due to enemy aircraft, 20 percent to gunfire and depth charges, 12 percent to mines, and the balance to a variety of causes including fire, foundering, and capture.   The lack of close air support from carrier-borne or land-based fighters was obviously the main contributory cause resulting in heavy losses to Allied naval forces from enemy air attack.

THE SINKING OF HMS ECLIPSE

HMS ECLIPSE accompanied by HMS PETARD, transported the 4th Bn The Buffs into the Aegean.   In the hours of darkness there would have been a sense of quiet expectation as the soldiers lined the rails: the naval officers on watch and the crew at other duty stations.   One can feel the salt spray and the smell of diesel oil as the ship cuts through the water at 30 knots and then slows as she passes through the Kos Straits; no warning of impending disaster. Suddenly, two violent explosions--a ship marked for special attention. ECLIPSE turned on her beam, broke in two and sank within three minutes. Fire and sudden death in a mined channel her epitaph.

The Captain of HMS ECLIPSE has provided a laconic account of the sinking of his ship. Detailed yet terse, the Captain's report provides a dramatic account of the death of ECLIPSE and of so many who were on board at the time.

ADW 199/1040   Office of Commander-in-Chief,
                                      LEVANT.
Commander-in-Chief,   11 November 1943
LEVANT.
     (Copies to;-Captain (D) Levant Destroyers.
               Captain (D) 8th Destroyer Flotilla.)

Sir,

1. I regret to report the total loss of HMS ECLIPSE under my command at about 0005 hrs on the 24 October, 1943.

2. At 0030 on the 23 October, I sailed from Alexandria having under my orders HMS PETARD, HMS EXMOOR and HMS ROCKWOOD. ECLIPSE and PETARD were each loaded with approximately 200 Army personnel (chiefly 4th Bn, The Buffs); and 10 tons of Army stores each. In addition, ECLIPSE carried Commodore P. Todd, DSO RN; Brigadier Stayner; and Brigadier G. Davy, CBE DSO, all of whom were destined for the island of Leros.

3. The intention was to pass through Rhodes Channel and Kos Straits during darkness and arrive at Palamat Kuku at 0030 hrs on the 24 October. ML's and various other craft were to meet HMS ECLIPSE amd HMS PETARD here, embark the passengers and stores from the two ships and transport them to Leros.

4. At about 1400 hrs on the 23 October, HMS ROCKWOOD reported that she had all the fuel in her forward tanks contaminated with water. This drastically reduced her endurance and made it important for her to return. This left me with HMS PETARD and HMS EXMOOR.

   HMS EXMOOR was not carrying Army or Stores and was not therefore essential to the operation. I considered also that with her maximum speed of only 23 knots she might seriously delay ECLIPSE and PETARD; moreover, it was undesirable to leave her alone in those waters that night or the following day. I therefore detached EXMOOR and ROCKWOOD to return to Alexandria.

5. The passage to Rhodes Channel via the vicinity of Kastellorizo was made without incident with the exception of one enemy shadowing aircraft sighted at about 10,000 feet in the direction of Rhodes, at dusk.

6. ECLIPSE and PETARD passed through Kos Straits at 2330 hrs, line ahead at 20 knots, with PETARD four to five cables astern. A signal was received about 1900 hrs stating that the Karabakla Channel was mined (Chart 1899) but this was subsequently cancelled. Information was also received that the wreck of the ADRIAS was ashore in position 3702 N 2716 E (CIC 231849C), and further that mines were known to exist in position 3659 N 2706 E (CIC 231741C) which was close inshore to Kos. Under the circumstances I decided to take a route through the deepest water in mid-channel after passing the Kos Straits.

7. At about 2359 hrs on the 23 October, in position 3702 N 2708 E, a very violent explosion occurred, apparently abreast No. 1 Boiler Room (though possibly slightly further forward) under the ship on the starboard side. The ship quickly took list to port which steadily increased until she lay on the beam and sank in about three minutes. Before sinking she was seen to break in two abreast the bridge.

8. From the evidence of my Executive Officer, Lt RBA Cantopher, RNVR, and other men aft, it appears that there were two explosions with about one or two seconds between. The first was not so violent as the last and neither magazine exploded as men escaped from the immediate vicinity of both. From the rapid way in which the ship sank and the severe damage which must have been done, it seems possible that two mines may have have detonated almost simultaneously, one by antenna and one by contact.

9. The majority of the men in the vicinity of the bridge were thrown overboard, though not many survived. All three members of the range-finders crew left the ship in this manner, severely

cutting their heads on the type 285 Aerials in passing. The range-finder was seen on the deck on the port side amidships by witnesses aft.

Three ratings escaped from the wheel house but two were severely burnt in a fire and flash, which was apparently caused from the oil fuel from the forward galley tank. These men reported that as they came out of the wheel house, the Captain's Sea Cabin (and possibly chart house) were in flames. Commodore Todd had left the bridge a few minutes before the explosion and is thought to have been in the wheel house or Captain's Sea Cabin, he did not go further below.

The fire caused explosions of ready-use ammunition at the starboard forward Oerlikon and possibly ready-use ammunition at "B" gun. One round apparently went off in the Oerlikon gun and caused a serious head injury to a rating (subsequently picked up) on "B" deck.

10. Six ratings escaped from the forward supply repair parties out of about 35. One man was thrown down from the upper mess deck to the Stoker's mess deck but escaped up through the ammunition supply hatches to the forecastle deck at "A" gun. In the forward mess deck, a large hammock netting at the after end was dislodged, falling over to port and blocking the port door.

The ERA on watch in the engine room escaped up the after ladder. One Stoker escaped from No. 1 Boiler Room. One Stoker Petty Officer who was in the air lock at No. 2 Boiler escaped with scalds to his back.

11. Aft, men were thrown heavily about but the majority escaped from the magazine and shell room. Two witnesses reported that "Y" gun was thrown out of its mounting; only three out of this gun's crew survived.

All lights went out (except automatic emergency) on the explosion, but it was reported that the lights aft came on again after a short interval. This allowed the two Brigadiers who were in the Captain's Day Cabin to escape. The watch keeper in the after HP switchboard did not survive.

12. Amidships, the soldiers were fallen in, a 100 each
    side, having just come out from forward mess
    decks. They were carrying their life belts and
    were receiving their final instructions for
    disembarking. Only 3 officers and 40 men
    (approximately) escaped. It is thought that the
    heavy casualties amongst them may have been partly
    caused by those on the port side becoming jammed
    against the guard rails by falling stores, as the
    ship listed.

13. Of the ECLIPSE ship's company only 6 officers and
    68 ratings are known to be safe out of a
    complement of 10 officers and 190 ratings. It is
    thought that there was a considerably larger
    number in the water at the time, but many may
    have perished while waiting to be picked up.

    HMS PETARD picked up 3 officers and 29 ratings,
    and about 10 soldiers before having to leave the
    scene. It is understood that rescue operations
    by ML337, another ML and an RAF rescue launch
    proceeded until about 0530 hrs on the 24
    October.(3)

14. The life saving torches (of which 40 had been
    supplied to HMS ECLIPSE for trial) proved
    markedly efficient, burning in some cases for over
    three hours. They not only were a mark for the
    rescue craft but gave the wearers considerable
    confidence and kept them together.

    Life belts for the soldiers had only been obtained
    by my 1st Lieutenant applying personally to the
    Army Embarkation Officer when the soldiers were
    coming on board. It appeared to be thought that
    life belts would be supplied by the destroyer in
    which they embarked.

15. It is considered that all Confidential Books and
    Signal Publications which remained on board (the
    Establishment had been reduced to a dangerous
    water set) were burnt or sank with the ship.
    Those on the bridge were in weighted covers; the
    remainder were either in steel safes in the
    Captain's Day Cabin or in use in the wireless
    office. No Telegraphists have been picked up.

    I have the honor to be,
         Sir, Your obedient servant,
              E. Mack, Commander RN

For this gallant ship, 126 of her crew and 135 soldiers, death came quickly. Such was the prelude to the 4th Bn The Buffs going into action on Leros: a double rendezvous with death.

By 10 September, in the Aegean the Germans had seized two Italian destroyers, four torpedo boats, five motor boats, six minesweepers, and fourteen small naval auxiliaries, to which twenty merchant vessels were added by the 20th. In the Adriatic 280,000 tons gross registered tennage (GRT) of miscellaneous shipping were seized. For the assault on Leros there were, in all, "twenty-five landing craft, thirteen escorts, and a covering force of two destroyers and four torpedo boats. Fifteen vessels were lost or damaged from a total of forty-four used."(4)

A German report made shortly after the action said: "England's sea power which is engaged throughout the World's seas, was not able to successfully defend important bases from where it had planned to put increasing pressure militarily."(5)

"On the night of 2-3 February 1944, Wellingtons of Thirty-eighth Squadron sank the 4,575-ton German LEDA bound for Crete from the Dodecanese and on the 22nd, RAF Beaufighters sank the 5,343-ton German LISA north of Heraklion."(6) These ships contained the greater part of General Mueller's battle group, which had fought for Kos and Leros.

Following the fall of Kos, all the efforts by the Royal Navy to reinforce Leros were futile. After 4 October, it was indefensible to incur such prohibitive losses among Allied ships. Had the Allies suffered far greater losses, in the defense of Malta or even Rhodes, they would have been better justified.

NOTES

1. Public Record Office, London, ADM 234/364.

2. Public Record Office, London, PREM 3/3/3.

3. Author's Note: Two of us went aboard the RAF rescue launch armed with a Bren LMG, tripod, and three boxes of magazines, to provide token AA defense. The launch cruised at high speed throughout the morning. Suddenly three low flying Ju 88s turned toward us. We traversed the Bren in their direction, but the Skipper felt it would be more prudent to run up the Swastika and promptly proceeded to do so.

4. CJC Molony et al., The Mediterranean and Middle East, vol. 5, History of the Second World War (London: Her Majesty's Stationery Office, 1973), 543.

5. Das Signal, January 1944.

6. Molony, The Mediterranean, 828.

The Army: The Battle for Kos

GEOGRAPHY

The island of Kos lies only four miles from the Turkish mainland and thirty miles south of Leros. The island is about twenty-eight miles long and six miles wide. The population at the time was estimated to be about 20,000: "The only port is the town of Kos on the northeast coast opposite the Turkish mainland. The airfield of Antimachia, eighteen miles away, is connected to the town by a road which runs the length of the island. The topography is rugged with the highest ridge reaching an elevation of 2,800 feet."(1)

PRELUDE TO THE BATTLE

The British garrison on Kos was built up over the period from 16 to 23 September. HQ company of the First Battalion Durham Light Infantry emplaned at Ramat David airfield in Palestine and were flown to Kos on 16 September. The battalion was on a very low scale, with virtually no support weapons. Seventh Squadron SAAF and Seventy-fourth Squadron RAF, both Spitfire squadrons, had arrived on the same day, but another two days elapsed before the balance of the DLI arrived.

Before the German assault, the Kos garrison comprised the following British formations and 3,000 Italian troops who had been garrisoned on the island since 1940:

* First Battalion Durham Light Infantry
* 2901 Squadron RAF Regiment 24 X 30-mm Hispanos
* RA, LAA Regiment 18 X 40 mm Bofors
* RAF Seventy-fourth Squadron
* SAAF No. Seventh Squadron
* Parachute Company Eleventh Para Battalion (The parachute company was withdrawn to Cyprus before the German assault on Kos commenced.)

Total 1,511 of all ranks. Combatant troops numbered some 800, among which, the infantry counted 460.

The Force Commander, Colonel LFR Kenyon, reported that within a few minutes of landing, a considerable state of disorganization and friction revealed itself; there was no British authority to deal with the Italian Command. British troops did not conceal their opinions of the Italians and there were frequent incidents, while British shipping entered Kos without previous notice or warning.

These circumstances were clearly not calculated to encourage the Italians to comply readily with the most important clause of the Armistice-resistance in the event of German attack. The political situation revealed latent difficulties between the fascist police, the Italian troops, the Greeks, and the British. Colonel Kenyon surveyed the Italian defense positions, weight of artillery, food supplies, transport, and state of the Italian garrison. He found that many guns were badly sited, the artillery troops were untrained, and there was a heavy incidence of malaria.

The Force Commander, who previously served as a staff officer on the Headquarters of Force 292, was concerned at the haphazard placement of a relatively small British force on Kos and the poor intelligence he had received with respect to German capabilities to mount a seaborne attack on the island. He assessed that the defending garrison needed an infantry brigade at War Establishment, a Royal Artillery field regiment, a field company of Royal Engineers, a squadron of tanks and squadrons of the RAF Regiment, to a scale depending upon the number of landing grounds operating, in addition to supporting troops.

By 2 October, three landing strips were ready in the Saltpans area six miles west of Kos. During this period, Colonel Kenyon had daily meetings with the other commanders on the island: W/C Love, RAF; Lt-Col Orme, CRA; and Lt-Col MacDowell, CRE. The Wing Commander did not consider that his four aircraft were filling any useful purpose beyond the strategic one of drawing enemy aircraft from Italy. On the other hand, as he was forced off one strip, he could not avoid using another, thereby giving away its existence. This directly affected the time the Army needed to produce a satisfactory number of landing grounds if the RAF was to be able to provide fighter cover for both Kos and Leros.

Meanwhile, octane deliveries for the RAF were straining the transport requirements of the island almost beyond capacity. There was an urgent need for 3.7 AA guns and more Bofors, while the meager reinforcement by aircraft diminished the prospect of building up an adequate fighter force. Kenyon made it clear that, in his judgment, the whole future of the Aegean operation depended on the British ability to hold Kos and to operate from Kos an effective force of fighter planes.

THE BATTLE FOR KOS

The Germans launched an amphibious attack against the island at
dawn on 3 October. Parachutists were dropped on Antimachia
while seaborne landings were effected at four widely separated
points from a convoy of seven landing craft and seven transports,
escorted by three destroyers and covering aircraft. The enemy
landing operation was assisted by thirty Ju 88s and 100 Ju 87
dive-bombers. Within a few hours, 2,000 German troops were
ashore with transport and supporting arms.

At "H" hour, 1 DLI was deployed with ninety all ranks on
Antimachia Airfield, seventy in Kos town, fifty guarding the
landing strips, while the majority, 250 were in reserve as a
counterattack force. The counterattack force "stood to" at 0445
hrs, and a coastal patrol was sent into the Saltpans area. At
0555 hrs, the Italian battery in the hills southeast of Gherme
warned that one large ship and two TLCs were approaching the
beaches in the Marmari Saltpans area. No previous warning had
been received from Force HQ of an impending landing.

A further enemy landing had been made at Capa-Foca by six
landing craft. Major Vaux, 2I/C 1 DLI, ordered C Company to
cover the approaches to Kos town. About this time mortar bombs
fell between Battalion HQ and the forward companies, the Italian
batteries on Gherme were being bombed, and telephone
communications with Force HQ and Antimachia Airfield were cut.
Lt-Col RF Kirby, CO 1 DLI, who had been in hospital, resumed
command and ordered A Company reserve into new positions.
Shortly thereafter, this company was subjected to a dive-bombing
attack by eighteen Stukas, closely followed by an infantry
attack, and suffered heavy casualties.

The enemy concentrated the attack against B Company and C
Company areas. From observation, the enemy was supported by two
50-mm anti-tank guns, and a number of 81-mm mortars. The
anti-tank guns were used well forward against strong points. The
enemy was firing tracer which proved effective and the HQ of one
platoon of B Company, 1 DLI was destroyed.

By 1700 hrs, the enemy had made a serious breach on the left
flank and followed up the withdrawal of the DLI. The British
troops were pinned down under mortar fire, and the harbor area
was being shelled. Kirby assembled his Company Commanders for
orders. At that moment two mortar bombs fell among the group.
The CO was hit in the head and the leg, OC HQ company was
severely wounded in the arm, and the QM mortally wounded in the
back. OC B Company was wounded in the leg.

After this, Major Vaux ordered all roads to be blocked and
covered by LMGs. The officer commanding A Company and the RAF
Regiment reported to Battalion HQ. Colonel Kenyon said that
there was a possibility of reinforcements in battalion strength
together with paratroopers expected at dawn. Vaux then gave
Kenyon his appreciation: The courses open were either to fight
on the line as held; to withdraw to a smaller perimeter around

the town and harbor; or to withdraw to the hills. Colonel Kenyon adopted the third course. After meeting Kirby, Kenyon found the Italian Commander, Colonel Leggio, and his Battalion Commander in a slit trench. Kenyon said:

> Leggio informed me that he had been out of touch with all Italian troops since 0600 hrs, with the exception of this battalion which comprised 300 rather than 800 men. Neither requests nor orders would induce him to order even a patrol to move to contact the 1 DLI or the RAF Regiment.(2)

At 2230 hrs, the Force Commander ordered the withdrawal to the hills. At 0600 hrs on 4 October, the enemy staged a full-scale attack on the former DLI positions, accompanied by a very heavy Stuka attack on the positions and the Kos town. The enemy then attacked the Italians at Gherme, who responded with MG fire from about four posts, but all the fighting ceased in a few minutes. At about 1300 hrs, Kenyon's group were stalked by an enemy detachment of about a dozen men. As soon as his party reached the southern slopes of Simpetro, they saw numerous groups emerging ahead and making off westwards. These parties were made up of the poorer elements of the garrison; many had thrown off equipment and arms.

Fatigue was beginning to tell and, in the absence of effective junior leadership, the men were gradually heading downhill. Kenyon dropped behind in order to locate DLI parties, but unfortunately missed them. By 1700 hrs, the Colonel was approaching Ascendio when, rounding a corner, he found a group of Italians. As Kenyon was negotiating for a guide, he was gripped from behind by a German sentry and taken prisoner.

By the evening of 3 October, the enemy had established local air and naval supremacy and were in virtual control of the island except for an area two miles in radius around the town of Kos, which soon became untenable. Wireless communication with Kos ceased after the night of 3-4 October. The German communique of 5 October claimed that 600 British and 2,500 Italian troops had been captured and that final mopping up was in progress.

The Germans attacked with the equipment of a brigade plus about 400 parachutists who dropped south of Antimachia. The enemy battalions were up to strength with support of one infantry gun and two A-Tk guns per company plus small- and large-caliber mortars. Colonel Kenyon mentions that a German sergeant informed him that he was on Kos four or five days preceding the landing. His main task was the early destruction of all main-line communications. He said that he had accomplished this task by 0600 hrs on 3 October. In drawing his conclusions, Colonel Kenyon said that, "there was an extraordinary dearth of any sort of orders or guidance from Aegean HQ in Leros."(3) After the war, the Force Commander wrote:

It was only when I reached London some 18 months
later, that I learned of certain facts which I
feel I should have known when I took the decision
to move into the hills.   With the virtual
impossibility of reinforcing Kos, and in the
absence of any intention to counterattack, it
should have been clear by about 1200 hrs, 3
October, that the time had come to cut our losses
on Kos.   The result of an order to evacuate if
received any time before about 1830 hrs, and for
which I had privately made plans, would
undoubtedly have resulted in saving the whole of
the DLI and one Battery, LAA Regiment.   As it was,
I am still convinced that it was my clear duty to
take the decision I did, which led to the total
loss of the garrison.(4)

It is probable that, in any event, the fall of Kos and Leros
before more commitments were made was not unfortunate if the
Mediterranean operations are considered as a whole.   The British
military force fought, worked, and with the few inevitable
exceptions, conducted itself in an exemplary manner.   One LAA
Regiment showed evidence of its skill and devotion to duty.
Colonel Kenyon said the Durham Light Infantry gave continuous
evidence of a very high standard of discipline: "Officers and
men in their respective spheres carried themselves with
gallantry, steadiness under fire, and determination."(5)
Total British casualties on Kos were sixty-five killed and
fifty wounded: "The Germans executed the Italian Commandant and
a number of his officers.   Their own casualties were eighty-five
men and two landing craft."(6)

NOTES

1.   The Durham Light Infantry at War, City of Durham Museum.

2.   Public Record Office, London, WO 106/2149, Colonel LFR
Kenyon.

3.   Ibid.

4.   Ibid.

5.   Ibid.

6.   CJC Molony et al., The Mediterranean and Middle East, vol.
5, History of the Second World War, (London: Her Majesty's
Stationery Office, 1973), 544-545.

The Battle for Leros

The future of the Leros task force was written in the sand, on the edge of the seashore; it was washed away, the water suffused with blood: one in four of the task force was killed or wounded.

GEOGRAPHY

The island of Leros is approximately ten miles long and varies in width from one to five miles. It falls naturally into three sections joined by two narrow isthmus. The whole is very mountainous and devoid of cover. A narrow valley runs from the northern extremity down the center of the island to its southern tip. Its continuity is broken to the south of St Nicola and north of Meraviglia by the low but prominent Rachi Ridge.

The island is indented by seven bays, each of which has good landing beaches. Elsewhere there are many places where the coastline is fit for scramble landings in calm weather by lightly equipped infantry.

PRELUDE TO THE BATTLE

At Kos and Kalymnos, the Germans had assembled a force of four F boats, thirteen I boats, five auxiliary naval craft, and a number of caiques; into these the enemy loaded the troops and equipment already assembled in these islands. Despite the earlier efforts of Allied destroyers and air forces, the Germans had succeeded in getting the bulk of their invasion flotilla in position for an assault on Leros.

At about 0130 hrs on 12 November, Allied aircraft reported two groups of seven and eight barges steering northwest from Kappari Island. It had been expected that the Germans would launch their assault in daylight from the cover of minefields at the northern end of Kalymnos. The Royal Navy destroyer flotilla leader considered that the forces were moving up to these bays and that he would be unable to interfere with them because of the minefield. Due to an erroneous appreciation in the CIC's

Operations Room in Cairo, it was not believed that these enemy formations might in fact be the assault force until it was too late to intercept.

In the early morning of 12 November, the evening assault force was reported by ML 456, patrolling off Leros. There is no doubt that, had the destroyer flotilla leader been ordered to intercept at once, the northern assault force might have been destroyed. The failure by the British to intercept these enemy forces after watching their progress across the Aegean is inexcusable.

The Germans acted with great determination and successfully called the bluff that Allied forces were a threat to them by day. By night the Germans hid their craft with great skill while their extensive air reconnaissance enabled them to know exactly where the Allied destroyers were and to attack while keeping their own forces clear. By 5 November, when the reinforcements had arrived, the British Garrison on Leros consisted of:

4th Buffs	360 all ranks.
1st King's Own	450
2nd RIF (with under comd B Coy 2RWK)	500
3 Bty (less one tp) 1 Lt. AA Regt RA	250
One Tp 18/25 Pdrs	50
Detachments 9 Fd Coy Sappers and Miners	50
" 47 DID RIASC	100
" 161 Fd Amb	70
" 570 AO and AD	70
" LRDG and SBS	100
TOTAL	2,000

Until the time of arrival of the Fortress Commander on 5 November, the relations between the Italian and British forces were unsatisfactory both politically and militarily. Less than half the total of 5,000 Italians on the island belonged either to the Navy or Army, the others being dockyard personnel and the remnants of merchant crews who had been torpedoed; of the latter, the majority were unarmed. This garrison was disposed mainly in the gun positions, which were sited on the highest peaks and designed chiefly for coast defense. The remaining Italian personnel were sited in infantry positions covering the bays of Portolago and Serocampo. Italian Headquarters were in Portolago.

The combined armament of the Italian gun positions was on paper impressive, consisting of guns varying in caliber from 150 mm to 20 mm including light and heavy AA. In practice, the fire power was highly ineffective; the majority of the guns were of very old pattern with worn out pieces and inferior sighting gear. The only heavy AA guns worthy of the name were six 90/53-mm guns for which there was scarcely any ammunition. No AA guns were served with any form of fire control instruments, and the coastal batteries had neither fire control instruments (apart from short horizontal base range-finders) nor any form, other than verbal, of range and bearing transmission. The system of communication was very poor; for the most part it depended upon single overhead lines, which were soon destroyed by hostile air action.

Until the time of Brigadier Tilney's arrival, Italian morale was very poor. The men had no confidence in their officers, and the officers had little respect for the British administration. The loyalty of at least a minority of the Italians was open to doubt, and the confidence that could be placed in the whole was equally dubious. Under these circumstances it was obvious that little reliance could be placed upon the Italian garrison and that the plan of defense would need to be designed accordingly.

It should be noted that German officers had been on the island until September. They knew the topography and existing defenses intimately, and the presence of agents or at least sympathizers of Germany was probable if not certain. The following were the main points of Brigadier Tilney's appreciation:

- Of the troops available only the British could be trusted; therefore, the dependable fighting force consisted of one British infantry brigade (supported by four 18/25 pdrs) upon whom would fall the entire responsibility for the defense.

- The German command of the air and the proximity of their bases gave them local naval control; thus their powers of reinforcement were many times those of the British.

- The uncertainty of the ammunition supply coupled with the German command of the sea and air meant that the longer the battle lasted, the greater would be the enemy's advantage. Therefore, the defense must strive for an early favorable decision, which meant aggressive tactics.

- If the enemy was denied the beaches in the bays, it could not land supporting arms; therefore, the beaches must be covered.

- Lack of transport and, therefore, of mobility would prevent the maintenance of a strong central reserve. Thus, the available forces would need to be deployed on a wider front than was desirable. This would aggravate the poverty of communications but was inevitable.

- Tilney's conclusion was that the enemy should be destroyed at the earliest possible stage of the attack.

The Commander's intention was to destroy the enemy at the earliest possible stage of his attack (1) on the sea, (2) on the beaches, and (3) on any bridgehead. The island was divided into three sectors and the infantry battalions allotted as follows:

North Sector	The Buffs
Center Sector	2 RIF (plus B Coy 2 RWK)
South Sector	1 King's Own (less one company)

All battalions were sited to cover the beaches in the bays, with one company in reserve in each sector. All units were to be ready to move into the other sectors and come under command of any particular sector commander into whose sector they might move. Fortress reserve (one company of the King's Own) was sited with the primary task of counterattacking any air landing in the North Sector.

- Medium machine guns were allocated as follows:
  North (twelve)-to sweep the beaches
  Center (ten)-to sweep the beaches and Mount Rachi
  South (eight)-to sweep the beaches

- Artillery-The Field Troops was sited in the central sector. The Lt AA Battery was also in the central sector with four guns sited primarily in a coastal defense role. Four 2 pdr guns were allocated to the northern and central sectors respectively in a coastal defense role.

- Italians-To ensure that they did not leave their positions and to avoid confusion between German and Italian troops, the Italians could only leave their positions at the risk of being shot unless they were wearing the distinguishing signal armlets.

- Fortress HQ was located on Meraviglia.

It can be argued that this defense plan had no stability in that the principal heights (Mount Clidi, Meraviglia, and Rachi) were not fortified and in some cases not even occupied.

Two factors from the outset were a very serious drawback to the defense: the first was the enemy's dominance of the air, and the second was the rocky nature of the terrain, which largely precluded digging defensive positions. Ultimately, however, the action called for probes coupled with immediate attacks on the enemy. The battle (on both sides) was offensive in nature; a battle of attrition rather than one of holding ground.

THE BATTLE

At 0530 hrs on 12 November, ML 456, which was out on patrol, signaled warning of an approach by enemy invasion craft. This ML engaged the enemy and eventually succeeded in returning to Alinda Bay and landing its wounded. The morning was dead calm and clear, and by 0615 hrs the enemy craft were clearly visible from the shore. Curiously enough, no enemy aircraft were yet on the scene and none appeared before 0730 hrs. The initial landings were made at 0630 hrs without air support. They took place simultaneously at Palma Bay, Grifo Bay, and Appetici, while a further attempt at Blefuti was driven off.

Enemy attempts at landing in the area of Blefuti were thwarted by shore batteries which sank one F lighter and two assault landing craft, and forced the remainder to turn back. One enemy company succeeded in getting ashore at Palma Bay; it was counterattacked by D Company 4th Buffs and, after a fierce fight, was entirely liquidated by midday with seventy prisoners being taken. The enemy made no further attempts at landing either here or at Blefuti.

By 0900 hrs, the Brigadier received a message indicating that Mount Clidi was being seriously threatened. This feature was one of considerable importance to the defense. It commanded not only the north-east promontory, but also the road and valley running through the center of the northern sector, and this particular area was being used as a dropping ground for supplies reaching the defense by air; it was also the area considered most likely for the landing of enemy paratroops and gliders. Mount Clidi also commanded the Alinda Bay area, and its capture by the enemy would most likely lead to the outflanking of the defense in the central sector.

In view of the importance of Mount Clidi and the urgent need of preventing its capture by the enemy the Brigadier ordered the Fortress Reserve (One Company of the King's Own) to move up in support of the feature. The reserve company arrived in the Clidi area about 1000 hrs, two platoons being sited around the guns and one being directed onto Pt 192. This platoon apparently lost its way and was mopped up by the enemy before reaching its objective. The first two platoons failed to hold what appeared to be a strong enough position and, by 1770 hrs, had been pushed back to the Italian barracks on the western slopes, leaving the top of Mount Clidi, together with the coast battery, in the hands of the enemy. Thus, the German operation LEOPARD was successfully launched with the Kustenjager (assault troops) landing in the northern part of the island.

At dawn on 12 November, members of the German First Battalion of the Second Parachute Regiment and the Brandenburgers emplaned at Tatai Airfield near Athens in forty Ju 52 trimotor transport planes, en route to Leros. Less than three minutes flying time from the DZ they were recalled to Athens because the situation with the initial assault force remained unclear.

In less than an hour, the paras emplaned a second time. Three hours later the Ju 52s were approaching Gurna Bay at wave top height. Climbing to 400 feet, the transports, now in line formation, dropped the paratroopers across the narrow neck of land lying between Gurna Bay and Alinda Bay. The Ju 52s were quickly enveloped by a barrage of flak from Bofors and small arms. A ball of fire engulfed one of the planes, but the remaining aircraft flew in steady formation with the parachutists making rapid exits into a hail of fire.

Laden with belts of Spandau ammunition, the German airborne troops dropped heavily onto the rocky ground. On the initial drop 150 were killed or wounded, but the remainder scarcely paused before going into action against the defending infantry (A Company 2 RIF and B Company 2 RWK). Moving out toward Mount Germano, the British troops saw parachute canopies draped over groups of dead German paras; perhaps fifteen canopies in the immediate area; fitting shrouds for a brave and resolute enemy. Before long the Germans had regrouped and assembled a deadly screen of resourceful paratroops to hold the Rachi Ridge.

Ceaseless attacks in cooperation between the Stukas, ground attack aircraft, and tactical bombers had a telling effect on the defenders as the battle progressed. Flares were fired directing the Stukas toward the exposed British infantry, who were immediately bombed and machine-gunned. As the dive-bombers turned off, the British were subjected to intense mortar attacks, suffering heavy casualties in the process. Within minutes, a fresh formation of Stukas was seen circling overhead ready to renew the attack.

The German paras were engaged with small arms fire by two RIF platoons and B Company 2 RWK (Captain Percy Flood, MBE) from Pt 36 and Mount Germano, and by two platoons of 4th Buffs from lower Quirico. They suffered fairly heavy casualties (stated by the Germans afterwards to have been 40 percent) both from this fire and from broken limbs, though they would have suffered more heavily had the men behind the medium machine guns been trained machine gunners. (The gunners were inclined to fire at the Ju 52s rather than into the box within which the paras were descending.)

The British troops in the immediate neighborhood of the landing, however, were so few that the enemy was able to reorganize without serious opposition, mopping up the two RIF platoons and establishing themselves in the narrow neck between Gurna and Alinda Bay. There is no doubt that the decision to land troops in this area was not only a bold move, but took the defense by surprise, since it had not been considered suitable for such an operation.

At about 1900 hrs, the Brigadier held a conference with OCs of the King's Own and 2 RIF and gave orders for a night attack to throw the enemy off the Rachi Ridge. Lt-Colonel Maurice French, OC 2 RIF, was to lead this attack using two companies (less one platoon) 2 RIF and two companies of the King's Own; 2300 hrs was fixed as H Hour. Events did not work out according to plan; the attack was first postponed due to the late arrival of the King's Own moving from the south, and finally canceled due to developments on Appetici and to the fact that one of the attacking companies had proceeded to the wrong RV and got lost in the darkness. The failure to launch this attack undoubtedly gave the enemy an unexpected opportunity to strengthen what was, initially, a somewhat shaky hold on the narrow neck in the center of the island.

At midnight on 12-13 November, a disturbing report was received from the Platoon Commander on Appetici to the effect that he was being hard pressed by enemy attacks up the eastern escarpment and that he required reinforcements. The Brigadier ordered the remaining platoons of that company to be sent to maintain the hold on Appetici, while a further platoon of 2 RIF was to be sent to strengthen the hold on Leros Castle. For some reason that was never satisfactorily explained, the move of the two platoons to Appetici was countermanded in a message from Fortress HQ without the Brigadier's knowledge. It was 0400 hrs before the Brigadier got these platoons on the move again after a further report on the now critical situation on Appetici. They arrived too late, suffering casualties in their attempt to reach the position, and the result was the loss of Appetici shortly after daylight.

The loss of Appetici meant that the enemy possessed a "point d'appui" on the right flank of the defense which threatened the main bastion at Meraviglia. An effort to recapture this feature obviously had to take precedence over a counterattack on Rachi. Accordingly, the Brigadier sent for OCs the King's Own and 2 RIF and gave instructions to Lt-Colonel French (who was also OC, Central Sector) to work out a plan for its recapture by a night attack on 13-14 November. French was told that he could count on all available men from the King's Own, who would form the major part of the force, and that he was to work out his plan in conjunction with OC of that battalion.

At 1800 hrs, the enemy launched the expected attack on Quirico and actually gained possession of it. An immediate counter-attack was made, and the feature was retaken with the exception of the Italian gun positions. In the meantime, OC 4th Buffs received orders from the Brigadier to recapture Mount Clidi during the night and to be prepared to move south the following day with the object of securing the northern slopes of Rachi.

As dusk fell on 13 November, the situation was as follows: In the north, the Germans had suffered heavily both in prisoners and other casualties, while the threat to Mount Clidi had been considerably relieved. In the area of Rachi there had been little activity but it was to be feared that the company of 2 RIF holding the ground between Appetici and Meraviglia was in trouble.

The Germans had captured Appetici but had undoubtedly suffered heavy casualties. Casualties to the British defenders in this area had also been heavy, constant bombing had taken its toll, a complete platoon on Appetici had been lost, the one in Leros Castle was in a precarious position, and the two platoons which had arrived too late for the relief had lost some of their members.

The Brigadier's estimate of the enemy strength at this time was 500 in the northern sector, about 400 in the Rachi area, and some 200 in the Leros promontory-a total of not less than 1,100 (it is now known that it was quite appreciably more than this figure). The British strength at this time numbered 1,200 (excluding RA, RE, and administrative personnel) and, of this number, 700 were in the Center Sector.

On 13 November, it became clear that the whole of the enemy's effort in the Aegean was being directed against the island of Leros. The Brigadier asked GHQ Aegean to send all available British reinforcements to Leros. GHQ agreed to send 2 RWK (less B Coy which was already on the island). One company was expected on the night 13-14, but did not actually arrive until the following night; it was hoped the remainder would be shipped across on the night 15-16th. Although it might be hard on these troops to put them into the attack within a few hours of their landing, it was agreed that the favorable opportunity might pass and, without their assistance, there were insufficient troops to defend the island; the essential prerequisite was to kill the Germans, not merely to hold ground.

The Brigadier returned to his headquarters at about 1600 hrs to ascertain from Lt-Colonel French how the plan for the attack on Appetici had worked out. As the situation had developed during the preceding twelve hours, it had become impracticable to employ any of 2 RIF on this attack, one company having been lost in the Gurna-Alinda bay area, one company already severely handled on Appetici the previous night, and HQ and one company committed to the defense of Meraviglia. It had, therefore, been agreed between OC 2 RIF and OC King's Own that three companies of the King's Own should carry out the task. Lt-Colonel French, knowing the ground better than anyone else, had, however, made arrangements to lead the attack himself with a guide from his own battalion accompanying each of the King's Own companies.

Briefly, the plan for the attack on Appetici was that A and D Companies the King's Own were to approach under cover of darkness and attack and clear the feature shortly after moonrise. HQ Company the King's Own was to follow up, organize the position and hold it against any further attack by the enemy. A and D Companies, having cleared the feature, were to withdraw as soon as possible to the area of Porta Vecchia (known as the Anchor), to be readily available for further offensive operation toward Rachi.

The attack was to be silent, and the weather deadened any sound of approach; the moon, being well into its third quarter, was rising sufficiently late to allow an approach to the objective under cover of complete darkness. "Advance to contact" should not have been a difficult problem, since a broad and well-defined track led up the side of the feature straight onto the objective, and those taking part in the attack had the advantage of being able to make a very careful daytime observation of the route from a commanding observation post on Meraviglia.

The attacking force arrived at the FUP unobserved, and the attack went in at 0200 hrs. It was, however, anything but a success. Although French himself led the way straight toward the objective, both A and D Companies of the King's Own experienced difficulty in maintaining direction and made little progress. Two platoons of A Company lost direction completely and were not seen again. First light found the attacking force in exposed positions still some way short of the objective, and the enemy, realizing the unhappy position of the attackers halfway up a bare slope, counterattacked down the hill inflicting severe casualties and causing the remainder to withdraw in some confusion.

Of the British officers involved in this attack 90 percent became casualties, including Lt-Colonel French, who was killed. His loss was a great one not only to his own battalion but to the brigade as a whole. He knew the island far better than any other senior officer, and his qualities of leadership, untiring energy, and painstaking thoroughness made him a very valuable officer. From A and D Companies of the King's Own, one officer and seventy men were all that remustered.

While the attack on Appetici was taking place, the Germans launched an attack on Meraviglia from the direction of Rachi. Although this attack was held, the situation at one time was threatening, since the brigade defense platoon was driven from its positions on the northern slopes of the feature and there was little behind them. The Brigadier was forced to recall HQ Company the King's Own from the Appetici attacking force, and the situation on Meraviglia was satisfactorily restored. It was unfortunate, if not unwise, to withdraw a company from the force attacking Appetici, but the attack never sufficiently developed for this company's role to be executed. The Brigadier was of the opinion that this withdrawal did not materially affect the issue on Appetici.

The Commander, therefore, decided merely to contain the enemy on Appetici and turned his attention to an attempt to destroy the German paras on the Rachi Ridge. With this achieved, he would be in a position to concentrate his force for a renewed attack on Appetici. This decision to attack the enemy on Rachi was further prompted by the fact that the German troops had undoubtedly become somewhat disorganized by the failure of their attack on Meraviglia during the night; an early counterattack therefore held out every hope of success. Orders for the attack on Rachi were given by the Brigadier to OC the King's Own and the new OC 2 RIF at 0730 hrs.

The attack went in at 0930 hrs with a great dash and determination on the part of C Company 2 RIF who got the enemy well on the run and captured a number of prisoners. Seeing the enemy to be in some confusion, the Brigadier ordered the advance of B Company 2 RWK and B Company 2 RIF along the low ground on either side of the ridge and then moved forward himself with an artillery OP party on to the southern end of the ridge. Unfortunately, the follow-up of the King's Own companies were neither as close nor as successful as it should have been, and they were held up by light automatic fire from groups of enemy who had remained underground and allowed C Company 2 RIF to pass over them.

The main point of such resistance was a feature known as Searchlight Hill, some 250 yards southeast of Pt 109. The Company Commanders of both King's Own companies were killed in the early stages of this attack, and this was undoubtedly a major contributory cause of the failure of these units. Not until 1100 hrs did they clear Searchlight Hill, and then all their efforts to clear Pt 109 failed. The end of the day found them still on Searchlight Hill, although they had been driven off this feature again at about 1300 hrs and had had to retake it late in the afternoon.

C Company 2 RIF who had pushed on found themselves in considerable difficulty, not having been followed up as they had expected. Toward the end of the day they managed to withdraw in rather a mauled condition to the area of Searchlight Hill. B Company 2 RWK met stiff opposition in their advance along the low ground west of Rachi but by noon had reach Germano where they contacted D Company four Buffs. They now came under command 4th Buffs and remained thus until the end of the battle.

The dawn counterattack on Mount Clidi put in by D Company 4th Buffs was successful, and forty prisoners were taken. B Company was then to have cleared Pt 192, and move on down to the north shore of Alinda Bay, joining C Company, which was being directed down the road to Alinda from Quirico. However, after clearing Mount Clidi, B Company was held up all day in the area of Pt 192 and withdrew back to Clidi in the evening.

In the meantime, the Germans had again attacked Quirico at first light and met with success, but they were immediately counterattacked and driven off by C Company 4th Buffs, which collected seventy prisoners. C Company then started to move down toward Alinda Hospital but met with determined resistance from every house in the valley and by nightfall had not made any appreciable headway; they were therefore withdrawn for the night into defensive positions about Pt 184.

During the day when it seemed apparent that the enemy was concentrated in some strength in the Rachi-St Nicola-Quaranta area, the Brigadier had asked the SBNO if bombardment of this area by destroyers might be arranged. Two destroyers duly arrived at dusk, steamed into the entrance of Alinda Bay, and gave a short but intense bombardment to the target area. The material effect of the bombardment may not have been great, but it is difficult to exaggerate what a heartening effect this inspiring display of outside help had on the defending troops.

The estimated state of strength on the evening of 14 November shows 4th Buffs to be down to 300, while 2 RIF had lost half their number, including B Company 2 RWK. The exact state of the King's Own was not known but they had suffered heavily and were undoubtedly more critically affected by the incessant bombing than the others due to their location in the Meraviglia area, which had become the center of attention for enemy aircraft. The defense had practically no rest from fighting for three days (although, neither had the enemy) and it may be considered somewhat reckless to have adopted and continued with an aggressive policy of offensive action.

For even the best troops, the effect of lying out in the open and being bombarded like sitting ducks, were very bad. It is scarcely an exaggeration to state that there was never a moment from dawn to dusk when the enemy was not bombing and machine gunning from the air. The speedy destruction of the enemy was imperative if the defense was to have reasonable hopes of dealing effectively with German reinforcements which were en route. As the battle progressed, it was evident that the enemy had deployed on Leros first-class combat troops, who demonstrated consummate skill, courage, and self-reliance in fighting for possession of the rocky slopes of the island.

Meanwhile, A Company 2 RWK (Major Robert Butler, MBE) arrived from Samos by minesweeper and was landed at Portolago at 2400 hrs 14 November. It was immediately ordered to rendezvous in the area south of Porta Vecchia. Battalion HQs and C Company of 2 RWK (Major MR Read, MC) were landed some hours later and were accompanied by OC 2 RWK (Lt-Colonel Ben Tarleton), who reported to Fortress HQ at 0600 hrs. It may be said that these troops were at a greater disadvantage, being landed on a strange island by night and moved almost at once into battle. To offset this, however, platoon and company commanders had had the opportunity of studying Mount Rachi, the ground over which they were to attack, from the OPs and Meraviglia, which afforded a commanding view of the Rachi feature.

The object to be achieved on 15 November was the destruction of all enemy in the Rachi-Quaranta area; thereafter the concentration was to be on the defense around Meraviglia. The plan of attack was communicated to all commanders during the night (by coded message to 4th Buffs and by runner through OC SBS, Major The Earl Jellicoe, DSO, MC, who succeeded in working his way to and from the northern sector). A Company 2 RWK, were to attack northwards up Rachi Ridge from Searchlight Hill and were to hold the ridge from its northern end to the center. First King's Own were to follow from Searchlight Hill and to hold the ridge from the center back to that feature. Artillery and medium machine guns were to stand by to support this attack by observation; no preparatory fire plan was possible due to the somewhat confused situation prevailing on the ridge at this time.

On a success signal being given by A Company 2 RWK, the Buffs were to attack southwards toward Quaranta and St Nicola and drive the enemy into C Company 2 RWK, supported by the available remnants of 2 RIF (the equivalent of a weak company). This group under OC 2 RWK was to advance northwards on a one-company front with its right on the road Leros-Quaranta and its left on the eastern slopes of Rachi.

A Company 2 RWK commenced their attack at 0830 hrs, but the supporting wave became seriously held up short of Pt 109, and not until 1400 hrs under cover of the last available smoke from the 18/15 pdr tp did they succeed, in a second attack led by Major Butler, in reaching this point. They suffered heavy casualties, including all their officers, and were soon forced to withdraw back to Searchlight Hill, as the King's Own would not release their LMGs to go forward to assist them.

By 1200 hrs, the Brigadier had realized that the first phase would probably not meet with complete success and warned OC 2 RWK that he had decided to put in phase two in any event. It was decided that this phase should be preceded by a preparatory fire plan and the CRA was instructed to carry this out in conjunction with the medium machine guns. Owing to difficulties of communication, this fire plan could not be laid on to permit phase two to begin earlier than 1500 hrs. The fire plan involved the expenditure of all the remaining ammunition available to the Italian coast guns that could be brought to bear on the Rachi ridge.

The artillery and MMG fire plan went well, but its effect was largely discounted by the fact that at 1500 hrs (H Hour for the attack), the infantry did not advance. As communication with OC 2 RWK had broken down, the Brigadier had to leave his command post to investigate the situation. It took him considerable time to find a serviceable jeep and driver. On arrival, the Brigadier discovered that OC 2 RWK had postponed the attack by thirty minutes due to the late arrival of the 2 RIF who were to follow up C Company 2 RWK. (A message to this effect had been dispatched to Fortress HQ but did not arrive until 1700 hrs, which further illustrates a state of disorganization.)

The artillery fire plan could not, of course, be repeated, and C Company 2 RWK moved into the attack at 1530 hrs, too late to gain much advantage from it. The company did, however, reach its objective and took fifty prisoners, though it suffered heavy casualties, including a near mortal wound to Major Read. It did not, however, make contact with 4th Buffs. The 2 RIF company that followed up became heavily involved with the enemy strong points, which had allowed C Company 2 RWK to pass over them and made very little headway. In fact, none of C Company 2 RWK was able to get back the way it had gone, and one platoon actually fought its way round the northern end of Rachi ridge and eventually withdrew down the road that skirts the western end of the ridge.

The Brigadier received no report from 4th Buffs during the day. Wireless communication had broken down and, being desperately short of officers and always hoping that a message would arrive, he did not feel he could spare an officer to make the somewhat hazardous journey. OC 2 RWK was now ordered to establish a defensive position covering the Quaranta-Leros road and to be prepared to renew the attack the following day with the assistance of his D Company, which was due to arrive from Samos during the night.

There was little more than a platoon and Brigade HQ left for the defense of Meraviglia unless the troops containing the enemy in the Rachi-Quaranta area were withdrawn; and to withdraw part of these troops would have served neither to secure the defense of Meraviglia nor to dislodge the enemy from Rachi. Thus, the weakness on Meraviglia had to be accepted. The east face of this feature was now the responsibility of Brigade HQ personnel under the G1 while the north face was under OC 2 RIF.

OC LRDG (Colonel GL Prendergast, DSO) was ordered to send out two patrols, one down the northern end and the other the southern end of the east face, both in the direction of Leros. They were to operate a limited distance from Meraviglia and, if they bumped the enemy, they were to simulate as much noise as possible without getting closely engaged, the intention being to cover the weakness of this front. The southern patrol did in fact encounter the enemy and 2 I/C LRDG (Lt-Colonel J. Easonsmith, DSO) was killed. It was most unfortunate that such a valuable officer should have been lost in such a manner, but the shortage of officers was now so acute that there was no practical alternative to his employment in this way.

At 0400 hrs on 16 November, the enemy launched an attack against the east side of Meraviglia and, by 0600 hrs, was threatening to overrun Fortress HQ. Every available man in HQ went to assist in the defense, and during the course of the fighting, the G2 and the SBNO's Flag Lieutenant (Lt Alan Phipps, RN) were killed and the G1 wounded. Brigade HQ was at the point of being captured. Consequently at 0645 hrs, the Brigadier decided to move his HQ with his senior staff officers and the SBNO to Portolago where he hoped to find the newly arrived D Company 2 RWK, (Major Bobby Flint, MBE) and use it to restore the situation.

At about 1600 hrs, a message was received from GHQ with the proposal to evacuate the Leros force on the night of 17-18 November, and that details would follow in the second part of the message. Brigade HQ was overrun before the second part of this message was received. Both the Brigadier and the SBNO were of the opinion that an evacuation was scarcely practicable and could only be effected at great cost in ships and personnel. Any idea of evacuation for the Italians was ruled out. It can now be stated that the Naval CIC Eastern Mediterranean confirmed this opinion and stated that it would have been impossible to evacuate any but a small portion of the British force on Leros, and then only at great cost.

At 1630 hrs, enemy machine gun, mortar, and small arms fire in the area of HQ became intense and the final assault on Meraviglia began earlier than expected. By 1700 hrs, it was discovered that it was impossible to get out of the HQ tunnel, since the enemy was standing over all the exits with light automatics and grenades. The discovery was made by the Brigadier himself when he endeavored to get out accompanied by the CRA only to be greeted with a grenade and a burst of automatic fire which, for some obscure reason, failed to inflict any wounds.

Brigade HQ was, therefore, completely trapped with all means of communication to forces outside entirely severed. It was unfortunate that this should have occurred without any warning. It seems that this must have been due to the fact that the handful of men left holding the eastern face of Meraviglia had become so demoralized by the enemy bombing and machine gun fire as to allow the enemy to occupy this vital feature without sending any word back as to what was happening.

The situation was now desperate. The Brigadier and what remained of his staff were caught like rats in a trap and all resemblance of control had vanished. Of the British troops outside, the force under OC 4th Buffs, which was moving toward Meraviglia, unaware of the situation there, numbered no more than 150 extremely weary men. The force under OC 2 RWK numbered not more than 200 and, not having received the Brigadier's last instruction, was marching in the opposite direction toward the north of the island entirely ignorant of the situation, while both the King's Own and 2 RIF had ceased as operative units.

Only two guns of the RA troops now remained in action with very few unwounded but exhausted gunners left to man them, and only ten rounds of ammunition left to fire. The Italians could be utterly discounted; the great majority had no spirit in them at all when they came into close combat with the Germans, and what morale they had possessed had completely collapsed.

On the morning of 16 November, a force of 250 promised by the Italian infantry commander had materialized as twenty-five men, all of whom had deserted before they arrived at the position ordered. The Germans, with their fresh reinforcements, now outnumbered the defense by four or five to one without taking into consideration their unopposed and overwhelming command of the air, coupled with their ability to land further reinforcements as and when desired.

In four days, eleven attacks were carried out on Brigadier Tilney's orders: one was of three-company strength, two of two-company strength, six of single company strength, and two of two platoons or less. Two of these attacks won local successes, five attacks gained partial successes, and four failed.

The possibility of either immediate or ultimate relief by Fortress HQ was negligible; only rifles were available, and only one man could cover each entrance at a time. Any active defense was, therefore, suicidal; the Brigadier stated he was prepared to accept this course of action if other considerations could be found to balance the defense. Far from balancing it, these considerations gave much weight to the conclusion that a suicidal defense would have been useless.

One possibility was to offer the capitulation of Fortress HQ and leave the rest of the defense to its fate. The Brigadier felt it was his duty to accept the greater responsibility, particularly in view of the order that had been received stating that there would be no evacuation, not only of Leros but of the Aegean generally. He did so at 1730 hrs 16 November 1943.(1) Thus ended the battle for Leros.

THE GERMAN BATTLE GROUPS

Elements of the Twenty-Second Infantry Division fought in the Polish Campaign in 1939 and in the Netherlands in 1940. In the period 1941-1942, the division was in Romania and was then committed to the Russian Front, suffering heavy losses in the battle for Sebastopol where Generalmajor Mueller was awarded the Knights Cross with Oak Leaves. One regiment served in Tunisia in 1943, while the balance of the division was posted to Crete.

In October and November 1943, the Twenty-Second Infantry formed a major part of the German Battle Group fighting on Kos and Leros. The division included IR No 16, IR No 47, and IR No 65 Grenadiers. At various times it was commanded by Generalmajors von Spaneck, Wolff, Keripe, Mueller, and Friebe. Generalmajor Keripe was captured on Crete by British commandos. (In the Aegean, Generalmajor Friedrich Mueller carried the rank of Generalleutnant.)

The Brandenburg Regiment was formed early in 1939 and contained glider and parachute units. The regiment was later expanded, and the Brandenburg Division was employed as a specialist anti-insurgency force used in the Balkans, and in particular, in Yugoslavia. II Fallschirmjager, II and III First Rgt BR, XV (Light), and IV Regiment BR were all involved in parachute drops on Leros.(2)

According to British records, the following formations of German troops were involved in operations in the Aegean in 1943:

Kos	2 Bn 16 Grenadier Regiment
	2 Bn 65 Grenadier Regiment
	Para Coy Brandenburg Regiment
	Assault Engineers
	2 Troops Artillery
	1 AA Troop
	1 Company Engineer
Leros	The Kos Assault Force plus:
	440th Grenadier Regiment
	1 Bn GAF Field Division
	II Fallschirmjager 2nd BR Regiment

      III Fallschirmjager   1st BR Regiment
      XV Light Kustenjager   4th BR Regiment

Shipping: Twenty-five landing craft, thirteen
escorts, and a covering force of two destroyers
and four torpedo boats.
Aircraft: 300 attack aircraft and ninety transport
aircraft.
Estimated landed strength: 2,000-3,000 men.
Estimated battle casualties: 1,000, plus 2,000
drowned at sea.(3)

NOTES

1. Brigadier RA Tilney DSO, After Action Report to the War
Office, 16 April 1947.

2. Bundesarchiv, Militarachiv (Freiburg, W. Germany, H. III,
10 June 1985.)

3. CJC Molony et al., The Mediterranean and Middle East, vol.
5, History of the Second World War (London: Her Majesty's
Stationery Office, 1973), 551-552.

Part III
Reflections

Combat Readiness:
For Whom the Bell Tolls

Following an outline on the "normative condition" of battle and
the legacy of death resulting from two World Wars, this chapter
provides a profile on the composition of 234 Infantry Brigade
and then focuses on the battle conditions experienced by these
British troops who fought with courage and resolution on Kos and
Leros in November, 1943.

A MEASURE OF MORALE

The use of uptodate technology and equipment, coupled with
tactical competence, are essential for success in battle.
Without the Spitfire, the Battle of Britain could not have been
won. Without the use of radar against the U-Boat menace, the
Battle of the Atlantic undoubtedly would have been lost.
Without air cover, battles on land and sea invariably were lost.
Meanwhile, maintenance of morale was always an indispensable
prerequisite in sustaining the conduct of battle.

A military formation has three distinguishing characteristics
that affect its performance: leadership, training, and
discipline. These qualities provide the foundation for the
exercise of motivation, skill, and endurance in battle. The
ability to fight in the face of casualties, confusion, and
fatigue is a measure of morale, without which, superiority in
numbers means very little.

The common denominator in war is stress, while the fighting
spirit demonstrated by a unit is a measure of its combat
readiness. Instant obedience coupled with self-reliance is a
sound prescription for a soldier. Inevitably some are better
than others; success often depends upon the prowess of small
units and even individuals. This spirit must be maintained
because each encounter reduces the soldier's chance for survival.

Military history is filled with acts of great courage, by both
units and individuals. However, setting aside the normal
element of risk, officers from battalion commanders to section

commanders frequently were killed in action, either because they lacked tactical skills or because they were required to be unduly visible in order to encourage reluctant troops to press forward in the face of enemy fire. The qualities of leadership, training, and discipline are also influenced by the ethos or character of a nation and reflected in its military history. The German soldier is brave and stoical; combined with his fighting skills, he is virtually unstoppable. The Wehrmacht placed great reliance on leadership by NCOs. Moreover, the German soldier is psychologically equipped and, by his training, stressed to kill. Similarly, Russian and Japanese soldiers exhibit these traits. But national character does not necessarily provide the behavioral answer in assessing the quality of troops.

In the French Foreign Legion, an elite force unique in all the world, over eighty nationalities are represented. Yet the legionnaire will fight to the last man. "La Legion Ses Morts" is a memorial to over 35,000 legionnaires who died fighting for France. Perhaps the differentials in the fighting quality of men have more to do with instilled discipline; a reflective measure of the endurance and sacrifices they are willing to make. Permissive societies, by definition, are inclined to lose the edge when it comes to endurance in the face of battle, some more than others. Not all countries are equally motivated by military values.

WORLD WAR CASUALTIES

In the First World War, France lost one and a half million men and the British Commonwealth a million more; 750,000 of whom came from the British Isles. John Terraine, a British historian writes: "World War I was represented as a unmitigated disaster for this country . . . Winston Churchill was haunted by the ghosts of the Somme and Passchendale."(1)

The trauma stemming from World War I and the Depression years was underscored by Neville Chamberlain's return from Munich in 1938, with "Peace in our time", and the catastrophe at Dunkerque in May 1940, when the British Expeditionary Force (BEF) was "flung out" of France. The French surrendered and the Vichy government collaborated with the Nazis; the mighty armies of France were rendered impotent; thousands of French servicemen were to spend the war in German prison camps. Only 7,000 soldiers of France were evacuated from Dunkerque under the leadership of Charles de Gaulle. Britain stood virtually alone.

Thus, not only was Winston Churchill burdened by his fears over a repetition of the scale of casualties in the First World War, he now stood witness to a debacle as the entire British Expeditionary Force of 300,000 men struggled back to the shores of Britain, demoralised, and in disarray. For Churchill, the British nation and, indeed, the entire free world, it was a nightmare; no one could think otherwise. The psychological effect of these events on strategic thinking and tactical performance of the Allies then came to depend upon three conditions which might otherwise be described as miracles:

- The destruction of the Luftwaffe by fighter squadrons of the British Commonwealth air-forces.

- The resolution of the Russian people to accept the fact that their country was to become the slaughterhouse of Europe; the cauldron where, at the cost of twenty million Russian lives, the German army and Germany itself, was brought to its knees, and

- The Japanese attack on Pearl Harbor which brought the United States of America into the War; ultimately to provide the dominant Allied force in the invasion of Normandy in June, 1944.

John Terraine, quoting Sir David Frazer says: "From June 1940, until the early summer of 1942, only four British divisions fought the Germans. (The Eighth Army in Cyrenaica). This is to be compared with the ninety-five identified German divisions encountered by the BEF on the Somme in 1916 . . . and the 131 identified divisions encountered in the Battles of Arras and Ypres in 1917."(2)

It was not until the summer of 1943, when Allied forces cleared the Germans out of North Africa, followed by the assault on Sicily and the Italian Peninsula, that significant divisional formations of British and American troops came to grips with German forces. Terraine observes: "Even the mighty endeavor of Operation OVERLORD only engaged less than a third of the total number of German divisions in 1944--and the British element in that performance was soon heavily outweighed by the American."(3) The Russian people were deluged with death, and the Allies prevailed.

The fluid nature of the war in north Africa, in western Europe and in Russia, also resulted in the surrender and capture of large groups, and on occasion, entire divisions. Frequently, the decision to surrender was taken at the command level. Only the German soldier could be expected to fight on, with no hope of winning. Among the Allies there was little attempt to train troops, other than commandos, paratroops, and special forces, in the art of "escape and evasion."

It is within this general frame of reference that we must consider the composition of the infantry brigade who fought in the Dodecanese, the battle conditions, and the tactical aspects of the action on Leros--in Roman mythology, the island of Diana.

234 INFANTRY BRIGADE

The 234 Infantry Brigade, which fought on Kos and Leros, was raised on Malta where most of its units had spent the first three years of the war. It was destined to make its final contribution in the Dodecanese following an interminable period of garrison duty on Malta which was long on endurance and short on everything else. There, the role of the brigade was essentially one of static defense. It involved laying concertinas of barbed wire, building stone sangers, digging runway dispersal strips and unloading the remnants of convoys which had run the gauntlet through the Sicily Straits. In some combination, these were ongoing tasks.

From the strictly military point of view, the infantry was engaged in sector defense of Malta's airfields and landing strips, harbor installations, coastal batteries and other sensitive positions. Companies assigned to the defense of Luqa, Safi and Taqali airfields were encouraged to fire their Bren guns at low flying armor plated Ju 88s.

Throughout the three year period, from June 1940 to 1943, the GAF mounted over 3,000 raids against the island, and to some extent, the garrison became dulled by this experience. Routinely, the troops, dispersed in platoon positions, were required to "stand to" before dawn and at dusk, in anticipation of parachute landings. "Stand to" would last for hours on end. The period of darkness in between, provided an opportunity for sleep among the persistent sandflies--sleep which was broken nightly by guard duties and by taking refuge in bomb shelters or slit trenches. For months on end, the troops averaged three hours of fitful sleep a night.

From 1941, the ration scale was progressively reduced until, by 1942, the entire garrison, as well as the civilian population, was near starvation level, until the siege of Malta was lifted in March 1943. The 231 Infantry Brigade (2nd Bn Devonshires, 1st Bn Dorsets, and 1st Bn Hampshire Regiments) prepared to leave the island to participate in the invasion of Sicily and then went on to land on GOLD beach on D Day. The 234 Infantry Brigade left Malta on 15 June, bound for Alexandria. The convoy was torpedoed in the Gulf of Sidra sending a troopship laden with 1,500 German POWs to the bottom of the sea.

In the Middle East, the month of July was spent in training at the Mountain Warfare Training Center near Tripoli, Syria. The best that can be said for this period is that the troops all became physically fit. In August, the brigade moved to Kabrit on the Suez Canal to practice amphibious assault landings. These exercises involved embarkation into landing ships followed by disembarkation via scramble nets into the waiting landing craft. A brief surge towards the sandy shore, where the coxswain promptly dropped the ramp, decanting his motley cargo of troops into three feet of water. The beach landing master added his contribution. Through a megaphone he bawls: "For Christ's sake spread out, you're close enough for sexual intercourse." So much for training in amphibious warfare.

In late August, the brigade moved to a tented camp in Insariyh, south of Sidon, and waited for the word. Someone quoted Winston Churchill: "Amphibious operations of peculiar complexity and hazard are about to commence." Perhaps the Prime Minister meant us, perhaps not, but his ponderous phrase was most apt in describing our immediate venture into the blue. Finally, the troops were free from the awful monotony of Malta. Now they were able to contemplate, with some sense of excitement rather than trepidation, the prospect of going into action. Regrettably, the action upon which the brigade was about to embark was short lived. What followed for most was more monotony, this time as prisoners of war, from which there was no escape.

BATTLE CONDITIONS ON LEROS

In the days and weeks leading up to the Battle of Leros, there was no attempt to orientate the infantry to the key physical features of the island, to reconnoitre the ground or to become familiar with disciplined tactical organization and manoeuvre. Two battalions were on the island for three weeks prior to the German assault, one battalion for a week; 2 RWK was brought from Samos and pitched into the attack in the final 24-hours of the battle. The dispersal of British units, hopefully to cover and repel the enemy on the beaches was tactically unsound. It served to weaken their fire power and impair communications at the same time.

No one was "clued in." However, one exception to the rule served to close the communications gap rather rapidly. It came from a company commander: "We think the German's will effect a landing and some of us are going to get killed." Silence. There was little to be gained by stressing the obvious. "Well, someone has to die." More silence. The Captain's assurances scarcely served to give his men a psychological edge. "Get fell in", and off they went.

Infantry action in the Dodecanese was a relatively straight-forward matter for highly disciplined troops; it called for a series of frontal assaults on rocky terrain. There was no classic offense or defense, no military architecture, parapets, sangers, revetments, or even slit trenches. It was a war of attrition--to kill or be killed. The action was fluid and constant; first one feature to assault and then another, invariably in the face of Stuka dive-bombers, mortars, grenades, and a hail of small arms fire. As the soldiers advanced, some were hit and fell, others continued to climb, and a few clung to the rocky ground, petrified with fear.

While enthusiasm overcomes hesitation, not everyone was enthusiastic about climbing the slopes of Mount Rachi. Brigadier Tilney remarked: "Highly trained troops of good quality without much battle experience are often more effective than veterans with too much battle experience."(4)   Two battalion commanders who refused to order their men into an attack on the Rachi Ridge were threatened with courts martial by the Brigadier.

The British infantry and supporting arms engaged the enemy when and where he landed.   For five continuous days they carried out attacking movements against highly trained paratroops and commandos.   Ultimately, attrition took its toll.   No matter how brave or resolute the British troops, their prospects were always hopeless.   Casualties reduced their numbers, limited supplies of ammunition eventually were exhausted, while dive-boming was incessant.   There was simply no way to relieve a worsening situation.   Meanwhile, waves of fresh German troops cruised off-shore equipped with 88 mm guns and the full paraphernalia of a new assault force.

The German assault troops on Leros were a tough and tenacious enemy.   They persisted in tactical offensive action and always had a logistical strategy in support of combat operations; air supply drops and assembly points were quickly established and identified with flag markers and smoke recognition signals. The Germans moved quickly from one position to another, but never retreated; they seemed willing to accept a high rate of casualties.   Their officers and NCOs exposed themselves to fire when directing an attack or defense.   They seemed indifferent to the British fire which they sensed was tentative; neither well coordinated nor directed.   The enemy was equipped with the MG42 which fires at rate 1,200 rounds a minute (compared with Bren's 500), Schmeisser sub-machine guns and satchels full of grenades-- all of which were used with deadly effect.

The action on Leros (an island less than 30 square miles in area), was not unlike a bullring, once inside, one had to perform.   With 5,000 British and German troops doing their best to kill each other, close encounters were to be expected.   The ratio of force to space was relatively high and the scale of fighting intense.   Setting aside the obvious futility of taking the high ground only to be dive-bombed off the ridges, the practical lessons were:

- Lack of air cover for the British troops.

- A poorly conceived tactical plan resulting in the dispersal of British units.   "Defend everything and you defend nothing."(5)

- The virtual absence of communications.

- The piecemeal use of British units in the attack.

- The superior quality of the German troops in bringing small arms fire to bear.

- The enemy's skill, tenacity and endurance:
  bravery and stoicism being the universal
  characteristics of the German soldier.

- The element of luck.

When Brigade Headquarters was overrun, the British were
ordered to surrender. With no air support, without supplies or
reinforcements, the Brigadier could see no value in building up
the casualty lists among his depleted units. Nor could he
conduct irregular warfare against the Germans; a mode of warfare
for which the British infantry had no training or skills. Given
the order to do so, many would have fought on but they were
instructed to bury their weapons. Thereafter, the terms of the
surrender took effect. As it was, one in four were killed or
wounded and the rest captured. In retrospect theirs was a
considerable achievement.

The Long Range Desert Group and the Special Boat Service were
also involved in the action throughout the islands. At the
outset, these special forces were intended to play a prominent
role in the Dodecanese. As a reconnaissance force, the LRDG was
employed in intelligence gathering, clandestine operations,
signals intercepts, and reconnaissance behind enemy lines.

The traditional role of the SBS was to provide raiding parties;
to destroy logistical targets, installations and key personnel.
These roles were not mutually exclusive and both units
complemented one another. However, when Kos fell and the German
assault concentrated on Leros there was little reconnaissance or
raiding to be done.

These special force units, the LRDG in particular, were called
upon to fight as infantry. This they did with their usual verve
and were decimated in the process. In the Dodecanese, the LRDG
lost more men than in three years of fighting in the western
desert. After the battle for Leros, the SBS was most effective
in rescuing small parties of British troops from the island, in
evacuating them to Turkey and, thence, through the escape and
evasion network to Kabrit. War Diaries and after action reports
describe the way it was on Leros:

> Our fighting men, though defeated, were not
> disgraced; the deciding factor had been the
> enemy's command of the air.(6)

> Tilney and his troops had fought a splendid
> defensive battle and came very near to winning
> it; unfortunately the standard of one of his
> battalions was not up to that of the others and
> failed him at the crisis of the battle.(7)

> The majority of British troops displayed dogged
> determination in defense and outstanding gallantry

in attack. The officers and men of all three Services in the Aegean deserve their laurels, won not by victory but by faithful obedience to orders.(8)

The quick surrender of many enemy island defenders was a surprise. Contrary to the German soldier who, where fate puts him, fights to the last bullet, the soldier of the Western Powers, (Allies) stops fighting the moment he recognizes there is no chance to win the fight.(9)

The British Command nursed a great distrust against the Italian troops on Leros, and as a consequence they were ordered to limit themselves to their defensive posts and never to undertake counterattacks. In my opinion such a degree of suspicion was not justified because in those critical days, all Italians were conscious of the kind of treatment they would be subjected to should they fall prisoner of the Germans. The stories of what had happened to their friends in Kefalonia, Kos and Rhodes were more than enough to induce them to fight for their skins.(10) (On Kefalonia [Scarpanto] the entire Italian garrison of 4,000 was executed by the Germans.)

Lack of performance is not generally due solely to the action of troops. Poor planning and intelligence, the lack of adequate resources and the inherent weakness of tying military operations to politically expedient provisions are all culpable in the assessment of "unsatisfactory resistance."

Winston Churchill said: "Kos fell after an unsatisfactory resistance. Leros fell after unexpectedly prolonged resistance."(11) The Prime Minister's comments on the fall of Kos and Leros encapsulate the contradictions which are inherent in all military operations. Inadequate resistance is always unsatisfactory. Perhaps everything other than an outright victory is ultimately unsatisfactory; Dieppe and Arnhem are cases in point. There is no virtue in defeat.

The Aegean was never a "vital mission" in either strategic or tactical terms. The commitment of 234 Brigade and the Royal Navy was purely sacrificial. There is nothing to read between the lines in describing the Aegean venture as a disaster. But it is the servicemen for whom the bell tolls.

NOTES

1. Terraine, John, Who Bore the Brunt?, World War II Investigator, vol. 1, no. 1., (Hounslow, Middlesex: World War II Investigator Ltd., April, 1988), 21.

2. Ibid.

3. Ibid.

4. Brigadier RA Tilney, After Action Report to the War Office, 14 April, 1947.

5. Max Hastings, The Korean War. (New York: Simon & Schuster, 1987), 97.

6. Christopher Buckley, Five Ventures. (London: Her Majesty's Stationery Office, 1954), 240.

7. Henry Maitland Wilson, Bt. Eight Years Overseas, 1939-1947. (London: Hutchinson, 1948), 182.

8. CJC Molony, et al., The Mediterranean and Middle East, vol. 5, History of the Second World War. (London: Her Majesty's Stationery Office, 1973), 559.

9. Das Signal, January 1944.

10. Jack Dimitriadis. Letter to the author, 3 September 1985.

11. Public Record Office, London, PREM 3/3/5.

Battle Casualties: Kos and Leros

The British war cemeteries on Leros and in Athens are tranquil places. Surrounded by conifers and olive trees, neat pathways link the orderly rows of white headstones, many of which, are engraved with naval, military, or air force insignia and the name, rank, and number of a serviceman killed in action. Some of the headstones simply record: "A soldier of World War II." These young men include the most definitive casualties from the Aegean. Others who were blinded, disfigured, or maimed lived on.

At the conclusion of operations in the Aegean there was a reckoning; more than 420 soldiers were killed: sixty-five British soldiers on Kos, 200 on Leros, and 157 drowned at sea. Nearly double this number of sailors lie at the bottom of the Aegean, while somewhere there are the remains of USAAF, RAF, and other Commonwealth aircrew who were killed in supporting the British lodgment in the Dodecanese: a total of 1,500 men.

To these casualties must be added 800 German soldiers, originally buried on Leros (now reinterred in a Soldatenfriedhof in Athens). Many of these, together with another 1,500, were drowned when their transports or landing craft were sunk, plus, Luftwaffe aircrew who were shot down over the Aegean. Padre Geoffrey Young who was mentioned in despatches for distinguished conduct on Leros, gave comfort to the wounded and dying, and organized the burial parties.

An estimated 4,500 were killed in the Dodecanese (1,500 or 33 percent Allied and 3,000 or 66 percent German). An untold number of Italian officers and troops were executed by the Germans throughout the Peloponnese and Dodecanese. Additionally, some 3,000 British troops became prisoners of war; all for a fleeting lodgment on a few small islands. A summary of Allied deaths on Kos and Leros is shown in Table 16.1.

Table 16.1

Allied Personnel Killed in the Aegean
October-November 1943 (Kos and Leros)

Service	Task Force	KIA	Percent
Navy	5,000	745	15.0
Army	4,000	422	10.0
Air Force	1,000	333	33.0
TOTAL	10,000	1,500	15.0

Based on known unit strengths and Commonwealth War Graves Commission records, figures for Army killed in action (KIA) on Leros are reasonably accurate. These include those buried with a named headstone and those buried without a known grave whose names are recorded on the Phaleron Memorial in Athens. The comparative unit strengths and losses for the Leros action are shown in Table 16.2.

Table 16.2

Army Units: Killed in Action: Battle for Leros, November 1943

Unit	Strength	KIA	% Unit	% KIA
The Buffs	500	177*	35.7	49.8
King's Own	500	45	9.0	12.6
RIF	500	22	4.4	6.1
RWK	500	18	3.6	5.0
RA	250	37**	14.8	10.3
LRDG	100	10	10.0	2.8
R Sigs/RE	50	3	6.0	0.8
SBS/SAS	50	2	4.0	0.6
Others	150	43	28.0	12.0
TOTAL	2,600	357***	NA	100.0

Standard Note: (NA) Not Applicable
 *135 drowned at sea (forty-two killed on Leros)
 ** 22 drowned at sea
***Table does not include the 65 British soldiers killed
  on Kos

The British War Cemetery on Leros contains 183 graves, among which 163 deaths were directly attributable to the action of 12-16 November.(1) The balance (thirteen RN, six RAF, and one Army) were killed at other times. From the Army contingent of 2,600 engaged in the battle the net number interred in the Leros War Cemetery is 163.

To these must be added those whose remains were not discovered when the cemetery was closed or who later died of wounds. Both categories are buried elsewhere. The probable Army KIA on the island approximates 200, plus 157 drowned en route to the island.

Based on scaled down battalion strengths of 500 men (officers 5 percent, NCOs 15 percent, and other ranks 85 percent) and from information contained in the CWGC registers, we can interpolate and reconstruct the distribution of KIA among these three groups.

Table 16 3

Comparative Distribution of Casualties by Rank

All Units	Offrs	NCOs	ORs	Total
Strength	130	390	2,080	2,600
Killed	43	65	249	357

These data show that one in three officers were killed, one in six NCOs, and one in eight other ranks. Attrition among company commanders and platoon leaders was very high. The King's Own War Diary records the death of fifteen officers on Leros and the rest wounded. The Buffs suffered apalling losses. Nearly 50 percent of the death toll resulting from the Leros action was suffered and endured by this battalion.

To this total must be added the wounded. By known count the wounded numbered 280: a ratio of 1.27:1.0 killed to wounded. Normally, the incidence of wounded is three or four to one; many from shrapnel wounds. However, on Leros, most British casualties resulted from well directed small arms fire. The ratio of killed to wounded was higher than is commonly experienced.

On the night of 13 November, (thirty hours after the initial German assault), eighty wounded were evacuated from the island. On 17 November (the day following the surrender), the author visited the hospital in Portolago. It contained about 200 British wounded, with beds in the corridors and stretchers under the beds. No estimate of walking wounded was made, and no information is available is respect to additional medivac operations.

From these fragmentary data it appears that at least 280 soldiers suffered moderate to severe wounds; more than 10 percent of the garrison. The combination of KIA plus wounded approximates 637, or 24 percent of the total sent into action. Most of the survivors became prisoners of war.

While the dive-bombing on Leros was constant, very few fatalities or wounded resulted from this form of attack. On Kos, however, the majority of those killed was due to aerial bombardment while defending the airfield. The majority of British casualties on Leros was due to small arms, grenades and mortar fire.

All deaths in battle are both poignant and unique. One death, at least, was preceded by a grim note of humor. Lt Alan Phipps RN, Signals Officer to the SBNO on Leros was with Brigade Headquarters on Mount Meraviglia when it was assaulted by members of the Brandenburger Parachute regiment. This naval specialist dropped into a slit trench occupied by Lt Jimmy James MC, Intelligence Officer, 2 RWK and promptly commenced firing his revolver at the enemy. Phipps remarked: "I always wanted a shore posting but never imagined it would be like this!"(2) Then came a burst from a schmeisser and he was killed instantly.

Immediately after the British surrender, Major The Earl Jellicoe, gave his parole to Leutnantgeneral Mueller in order to search for the body of Alan Phipps, who was his close friend. Lt Landry of the Brandenburgers was awarded the Knights Cross (Ritter Kreuz) for storming Meraviglia, the only Ritter Kreuz awarded for the Leros campaign.

PRISONERS OF WAR AND "THE ORIENT EXPRESS"

So ended the battles for Kos and Leros. A significant number of survivors from the Dodecanese (2,000-3,000) were shipped in freighters to Pireaus. The British troops were allowed to stay on deck--the Italian officers were forced down vertical ladders into the holds; German rifle butts smashed their fingers ensuring a rapid descent and the holds were then battened down.

Upon arrival in Pireaus, the British column was marched through Athens, watched by a sympathetic crowd of Athenians. The intrepid Captain Olivey, LRDG, stepped out of the line of march and merged into the crowd: for the rest, two weeks in a transit prison. At the railroad station lines of boxcars, festooned with barbed wire stood ready--doors opened, into which were herded groups of forty prisoners. Each man was provided with a three-day ration--a hunk of grey bread. The doors were slammed shut and bolted from the outside, and the train pulled out.

For fifteen days and nights the prison train clanked its way through Greece, Yugoslavia, Bulgaria, and Hungary. Arriving at the train station in Budapest, after a journey of twelve days, the troops received one-half inch of potato soup in their mess tins. The journey resumed. Three days later a ring of lights--Stalag VIIA, Mosburg, Germany. The doors to the boxcars were flung open and the lice-ridden, emaciated troops emerged from a month of hunger and privation, and staggered into the cold dawn. It was Christmas Eve 1943.

NOTES

1. Commonwealth War Graves Commission, <u>British War Cemetery Register</u>, Leros, Dodecanese.

2. Captain J James CB, MC., in a conversation with the author, 1 December 1985.

Honors and Awards

The distribution of Honors and Awards to members of 234 Infantry Brigade who were on Leros is recorded in a supplement to the London Gazette, dated 13 September 1945.(1) The distribution of decorations to the four infantry battalions engaged in the battle is shown in Tables 17.1 and 17.2. A total of twenty-three medals and forty-eight mentioned in despatches were awarded. The distribution of these awards was as follows: officers, 42 percent; NCO's 27 percent; and other ranks 31 percent. Thus, those in a leadership capacity attracted 69 percent of the total.

Table 17.1

Honors and Awards by Regiment: Leros, November 1943

Unit	DSO	MC	MCBar	MM	MID	Total	%
Royal Irish Fusiliers		3		3	22	28	39.4
The Buffs (Royal East Kents)	1	4	1	5	13	24	33.8
Royal West Kents		6			7	13	18.3
King's Own Regiment					6	6	8.5
Totals	1	13	1	8	48	71	100.0

Source: London Gazette, 13 September, 1945.

The seventy-one Honors and Awards shown do not take into account any others that may have been promulgated in other issues of the London Gazette. The summary is in respect to the four infantry regiments who were engaged in action. It does not include corps troops or special forces. Table 17.2 shows the distribution of awards by rank.

Table 17.2

Honors and Awards by Rank: Infantry Regiments:
Leros, November 1943

Award	LCol	Maj	Capt	Lt	WO	Sgt	Cpl	L/C	Pte	Total	%
DSO	1									1	1.4
MC		3	3	7						13	18.3
MCBar				1						1	1.4
MM						1	2	1	4	8	11.3
MID	1	1	5	8	4	6	3	2	8	48	67.6
Totals	2	4	8	16	4	7	5	3	22	71	100.0

Source: Same as Table 17.1

The Second Battalion Royal Irish Fusiliers received 39 percent of the awards followed closely by Fourth Battalion The Buffs, with 33.8 percent. On average, the highest percentage of awards was earned by The Buffs since, as noted, this battalion was well under strength due to the losses suffered when HMS ECLIPSE went down (carrying 135 officers and men).

Only six awards were made to the King's Own. In view of the casualties sustained by this battalion (24 percent of the battle), the small number of awards is surprising. Most of the King's Own officers were killed or wounded. This attrition suggests that many actions deserving an award were never reported.

Among the twenty-three medals, fifteen were awarded to officers and eight to other ranks. Of the four battalion commanders, Lt-Col Douglas Iggulden, Fourth Battalion The Buffs, received the DSO. Among the MIDs, fifteen went to officers and thirty-four to other ranks. Lt-Col Maurice French, 2n Bn RIF, was awarded a posthumous MID. In the case of Lt-Col French, Brigadier Tilney wrote:

> I recommended him for a posthumous "Mention In Despatches" which is the utmost that one can do for one who died in circumstances when the award of the Victoria Cross is only forgone for the lack of positive evidence to support it. I believe he probably earned it."(2)

Sergeant Doyle commanding the Pioneer Platoon, was called to a AP minefield near the beaches where he found a Greek woman had walked into the minefield and was severely wounded. Her legs were touching the trip wires of other unexploded mines. Despite the fact that she was moving her body and the mines were likely to explode at any moment, Sergeant Doyle crawled into the minefield, made the mines safe, and carried the woman to safety.

During the afternoon of 12 November, Lieutenant Gore-Booth was mortally wounded on Appetici while gallantly leading a patrol around the right flank. Fusilier McKeever, though himself wounded, made a brave attempt to carry Lt Gore-Booth back to Company HQ under heavy enemy fire. Doyle, McKeever and Gore-Booth (posthumous) received MIDs.(3)

A Military Cross, which more properly should have been a DSO, was awarded to Major Robert Butler MBE, 2 RWK. This company was sent from Samos on 13 November, but due to the appalling visibility and sea conditions and to a navigational error, failed to reach Leros during that night and was obliged to lie up in Turkish waters during the 14 November, eventually reaching Portolago (Lakki) at 11:00 p.m. Following a briefing by the Brigadier, the company was ordered to capture Pt 100 on the Rachi Ridge, which a composite battalion had failed to capture on the previous day.

Zero hour was set for 0830 hrs. A Company advanced from the startline behind Pt 103, in a square formation, with Lt Groom's and Lt John's platoons ordered to move forward with "fire and movement" on the right, and Lt Hewett's platoon supported by company headquarters with two LMGs on the left. When Lt Hewett's platoon was getting on to the objective, the company commander saw Lt Hewett killed, and moved forward quickly to coordinate the occupation of the company's objective.

The fire power of the enemy's LMGs was, however, then redirected onto the second flight of A Company, causing heavy casualties, including CSM Spooner killed and Lts Groom and John wounded. Major Butler could be seen moving into the center of the enemy's position just short of an irregular line of enemy machine gun positions. He then took up a fire position to neutralize the enemy. Butler survived a mortar bombardment by a detachment of the RIF, and although he received a wrist wound, he managed to make a dash back to his own men who were pinned down. This officer immediately formulated a plan for a second assault on the enemy's positions.

This second attack by A Company went in under effective smoke, a mortar bombardment from the RIF, and the raked fire of A Company's eleven LMGs, which allowed the two reformed platoons to reach their objective. Many casualties were suffered during the fighting, including Major Butler who received a second bullet wound which paralyzed his right leg, and Captain Grimshaw, who received a severe wound in the wrist.

The enemy counterattacked immediately with heavy fire and Major Butler sent a runner back to speed up the arrival of his LMGs which by then should have been on the move. The runner returned with the message that the King's Own would not allow these guns to be moved from positions in their forward defended localities. It seemed impossible for the remnants of A Company, which by now numbered twelve men, to hold the Rachi Ridge armed only with rifles. Major Butler then called for stretcher bearers for the wounded and withdrew the survivors to the comparative shelter of Pt 103, using mainly the dead ground on the west side of the ridge.(4) Table 17.3 shows comparative ratios of honors and awards between officers and other ranks.

Table 17.3

Comparative Ratios of Honors and Awards:
Infantry: Officers and Other Ranks: Leros, November 1943

Rank	No.	Medal	Ratio	MID	Ratio	Total	Ratio
Officers	130	15	1:9	15	1:9	30	1:4
Other Ranks	1,715	8	1:214	33	1:52	41	1:42
Total	1,845	23	N/A	48	N/A	71	1:26

Standard Note: (N/A) Not Applicable.

Source: From Tables 17.1 and 17.2.

Awards to officers are shown to be tenfold over those awarded to other ranks, while the proportion of officers to other ranks was in a ratio of 1:13.

In World War II, the distribution of gallantry awards in the British Forces averaged 1:250. In general, the infantry, which absorbed about 85 percent of the casualties in battle, represented only 15-20 percent of the forces engaged. On Leros, however, the infantry was the predominant arm and the primary force.

The ratio of awards (1:26), for the infantry on Leros is, therefore, a measure of recognition for a hard fought action. It should also be noted that there was a lapse of eighteen months between the battle and the submission of citations, with the interval between being spent as prisoners of war.

The survivors of the Brandenburger Regiment, which totaled some 300 officers and men, received immediate awards of eight Iron Cross I, sixty Iron Cross II, and one Knights Cross.(5) The Iron Cross in various classes is awarded irrespective of rank, as is the Croix de Guerre. The latter is awarded whenever a citation is made for bravery.

NOTES

1. Supplement to the London Gazette, (London: Her Majesty's Stationery Office, 13 September 1945.)

2. Brigadier RA Tilney. Letter to Mrs. Diana French, 1 January 1946.

3. Author's note: Until 17 April 1979, only two categories of Award could be made posthumously; the VC and MID. The rule has since been changed and additionally the following Decorations

can now be awarded posthumously; DSC, MC, DFC, DCM, CGM, MM, DFM, AFC, AFM, RRC and ARRC. Source: Letter to the author dated 4 June 1985, from MOD (MS 1b). This change in the categories of Posthumous Awards was first recommended in 1949 and promulgated 30 years later.

In reference to the grant of an "immediate" award for a "mention in despatches", a recent letter from MOD (MS 1b) offered the following opinion: ". . . some demonstrable form of recognition is justified to indicate an award [which] must in logic rank as superior to a campaign, long service, or commemorative medal."

4. Lt-Col Robert Butler. Personal account given to the author in a letter 4 June 1985.

5. Das Signal, January 1944.

Part IV
Appendices

Appendix I
Dodecanese Islands

Form Adopted	Greek(1)	Classical(1)	Italian	Turkish
Alimnia			Alimnia	Alimnia
Arki			Archi	Arki
Kalymnos	Kalymnos		Calino	Kalimnos
Kasos	Kasos		Casos	Cascoit
Kastellorizo	Kastellorizo	Megiste	Castelrosso	Meis
Chalkia		Chaklia	Calchi	Harki
Kos	Kos		Coo	Istankioi
Gaidaro			Gaidaro	
Levita		Lebinthos	Levita	
Leros			Lero	Leros
Nisyros			Nisiro	Ingirli, Nisiros
Patmos			Patmo	Patmos
Piscopi		Telos	Piscopi	Tilos, Gedaro
Rhodes	Rhodes		Rodi	Rodos
Scarpanto		Karpathos	Scarpanto	Kerpe
Stampalia	Stampalia (Astropalia)	Astypalaia	Stampalia	Ustrupalia, Astropalya
Symi			Simi	Sumbeki

(1)Where no form is given in these columns, the form is the same as in the preceding column.

Appendix II
Diary of Events

Conference and Diary Notes of Events that had a bearing on Operations in the Aegean.

27 November 1942. Joint Intelligence Committee (JIC) considers opportunities for Allied action in the Balkans.

January 1943. Casablanca Conference. Allied strategy that limited war in Japan in favor of Mediterranean operations.

12 February 1943. Wilson directed by British COS to prepare for amphibious operations in the eastern Mediterranean.

19 March 1943. Joint Planners to consider what plans should follow operation HUSKY (the invasion of Sicily).

17 April 1943. Joint Planners recommend Allies should invade toe of Italy.

20 April 1943. Operation HARDIHOOD discussed. (Plans to bring Turkey into the war.)

3 May 1943. Plans made in the event Italy collapsed before or as result of HUSKY.

12-25 May 1943. Trident Conference, Washington DC. Priority for OVERLORD (cross-Channel invasion, May 1944) and ANVIL (invasion of southern France).

10 July 1943. Allies land in Sicily.

20 July 1943. General Wilson identifies three versions of ACCOLADE: (1) walk in to Rhodes and other islands if Italians collapsed and Germans withdrew; (2) a "quick" opportune ACCOLADE if Italians collapsed but Germans were standing firm; and (3) a

full ACCOLADE against Italian and German opposition.

1 August 1943. General Wilson identifies his resources and needs for a "quick" ACCOLADE.

2 August 1943. Standstill Order. British COS authorized eight LSI earmarked for India to be retained in the Middle East.

5 August 1943. General Wilson asks General Eisenhower for support to arrive in Middle East by 14-15 August, to include

eight ships and craft, four squadrons of P-38s (Lightnings), transport aircraft, and troops.

7 August 1943. Eisenhower agrees to release troops and some shipping but not the P-38s or transport aircraft.

12 August 1943. Eisenhower, Alexander, and Tedder reconsider commitment made on 7 August and now state ACCOLADE should be abandoned for the present.

17 August 1943. Quadrant Conference, Quebec. Sets limits on operations in the Aegean.

18 August 1943. Revocation of Standstill Order. COS to VCOS: "Agreement with USJCOS that operations in the Mediterranean will be carried out with forces allotted at Trident except so far as these may be varied by Combined Chiefs of Staff."

21 August 1943. Ships previously authorized to be retained in Middle East now ordered to disperse to Indian Ocean.

23 August 1943. Wilson signals to Eisenhower that he is loading the task force for ACCOLADE.

26 August 1943. Eisenhower warns Wilson that he will soon require Eighth Indian Division in central Mediterranean. The Eighth Division is ordered to central Mediterranean.

31 August 1943. Wilson informs Eisenhower: "Any enterprise against Rhodes or Crete except as unopposed walk-in is now impossible."

3 September 1943. Allies invade Italy, code name BAYTOWN. Eighth Army at Reggio di Calabria.

7 September 1943. Wilson formulates another plan. Following Armistice with Italy, Wilson embarks on small operations to Kastellorizo, Kos, Leros, and Samos. Inter-Service Mission to Rhodes to treat with General Scaroina and Admiral Campioni in "rounding up" the 7,000 German Assault Division based on Rhodes.

If favorable, intention was to land 234 Infantry Brigade in three merchant ships, not assault loaded. Success would depend upon use of Rhodes harbor and the airfields on which one or two squadrons of Spitfires would be ready to land.

8 September 1943. Italy surrenders.

9 September 1943. Fifth US Army assaults Salerno, Operation AVALANCHE.

9 September 1943. Germans on Rhodes ordered to resist all attacks from any source.

9-10 September 1943. Rodell Mission. Major The Earl Jellicoe, SBS, to meet General Scaroina and Admiral Campioni on Rhodes.

10 September 1943. German General Klemann seizes General Scaroina and attacks Regina Division on air and land.

11 September 1943. Admiral Campioni orders the Italian garrison on Rhodes to capitulate to the Germans.

13 September 1943. Churchill, en route to Halifax, signals to Wilson: "The capture of Rhodes by you at this time with Italian aid would be a fine contribution to the general war."

14 September 1943. Wilson, Personal for Prime Minister: "I am sending troops to occupy Kastellorizo, Kos, Leros and Samos. LRDG and SBS also to Patmos, Symi and Lemnos. B Coy 2 RWK to Kastellorizo."

17 September 1943. First Battalion Durham Light Infantry, plus 2909th Squadron RAF Regiment with light AA weapons and Seventh Squadron South African Air Force with seven Spitfires to Kos.

21 September 1943. Wilson submits to British COS his plan to put a garrison, Second Battalion Royal Irish Fusiliers, into Leros.

23 September 1943. Second Battalion Royal West Kent Regiment (minus B Company) to Samos.

24 September 1943. German Assault Group assemble for attack on Kos and formulate plan, code name LEOPARD, for attack on Leros.

1 October 1943. In consultation with Eisenhower, British COS authorizes CIC Middle East to capture Rhodes before the end of October.

3 October 1943. Kos assaulted by German Battle Group. Falls within twenty-four hours after what Churchill described as "An unsatisfactory resistance."

6 October 1943. General Sir Alan Brooke, CIGS: "There is a grave danger that we shall find ourselves drawn into an amphibious campaign in the eastern Mediterranean leading into Greece which would absorb resources which might be badly needed in Italy."

The First Sea Lord, Sir Andrew Cunningham: "The use of Turkish airstrips while enabling us to provide a valuable support for offensive operations against the islands, would not help us a great deal to defend Leros and Kos on account of the distances involved and the absence of an adequate warning system."

7 October 1943. Churchill asks Roosevelt to reconsider his objections, saying, "Nine landing craft, six months before they will be needed for OVERLORD is all I ask."

9 October 1943. Roosevelt to Churchill: "As I see it, it is not merely the capture of Rhodes, but it must be of necessity, and it must be apparent to the Germans, that we intend to go further. Otherwise Rhodes will be under the guns of Kos and Crete. Strategically, if we get the Aegean islands, I ask myself where do we go from there, and vice versa, where would the Germans go if for sometime they retained possession of the islands?"

9 October 1943. Prime Minister to Wilson: "You should press most strongly at the conference for ACCOLADE (Rhodes) 'Storm Rhodes.' Demand what is necessary and consult with Alexander."

10 October 1943. Germans decide to reinforce army in Italy and fight a main battle south of Rome.

10 October 1943. Churchill to Eden: "Is there no hope? If nothing can be done you should consult with Wilson whether Leros garrison should not be evacuated to Turkey. We cannot go on indefinitely with costly special Naval operations once it is clear that nothing can be done to restore the situation."

10 October 1943. Churchill to Alexander: "You should now try to save what we can from the wreck."

10 October 1943. Prime Minister to Foreign Secretary: "We (sic) You should now try to save what we can from the wreck." Admiral Cunningham expressed the opinion Kos/Leros combination could be held on a self-contained basis. He now telegraphs: "Kos cannot be recaptured without use of Turkish airfields." [In the Prime Minister to Foreign Secretary version, the original text reads: "We should . . .", not "You should . . ." The amended text is initialed WSC, (CAB 120.)]

10 October 1943. Prime Minister to Wilson: "Cling on if you possibly can. Talk it over with Eden and see what help you can

get from the Turks. If after everything has been done you are forced to quit I will support you, but victory is the prize."

10 October 1943. Wilson to Churchill: "I agree that Alexander's operations ought to have the whole of available resources."

10 October 1943. La Marsa Conference: "If Rhodes is not captured and held, there is no chance of restoring local air situation sufficient to allow surface forces and maintenance shipping to defend and maintain the islands we still hold." (Leros and Samos)

Air Chief Marshal Sir Arthur Tedder: "It would be necessary to employ all P-38 (Lightning) aircraft in the Mediterranean. Even adding carrier-borne aircraft which might be available we consider this cover quite inadequate. We must concentrate on the Italian campaign. ACCOLADE must be postponed."

12 October 1943. Eden meets with Wilson and Middle East Commanders in Cairo: "No chance of success to recapture Kos. We must keep our eyes fixed on HANDCUFF (Rhodes). We are in no doubt we should hold on to Leros."

14 October 1943. Churchill to Wilson: "I am very pleased with the way you used such poor bits and pieces as were left to you. Nil desperandum."

Prime Minister to Wilson: "For your eyes alone and for the Secretary of State for Foreign Affairs to see if still in Cairo: 'Keep Leros safely.'"

22 October 1943. Fourth Battalion The Buffs embark for Leros in HMS ECLIPSE and HMS PETARD.

22-23 October 1943. HMS ECLIPSE hits a mine and is sunk with the loss of 135 officers and men from Fourth Battalion The Buffs plus more than 125 of the ship's crew.

31 October 1943. Air Chief Marshal Sir Arthur Tedder: "We are being pressed to throw good money after bad. The situation is fundamentally unsound."

1 November 1943. Prime Minister to Foreign Secretary in Moscow: "You should try to grip the Leros--Samos situation. This is in a most hazardous plight but the prize is worth struggling for."

1 November 1943. For the Prime Minister from Anthony Eden: "I again dwelt on the fact that airfields in southwest Anatolia were an urgent operational requirement not only to avert disaster at Samos and Leros but also to enable us to capture and

maintain Rhodes which in our view is the key to the Aegean. Molotov asked whether the United States delegation would be prepared to march with us in this matter?" I said, "I could not be certain."

5 November 1943. First Battalion King's Own Regiment arrives in Leros.

7 November 1943. Turkish Foreign Secretary, M. Numan, rejects Eden's demands for use of airfields and a commitment to enter the war.

10 November 1943. From War Cabinet Office, London, to Joint Staff Mission, Washington: "Turkish Government is now considering the proposal put to them by Foreign Secretary in Cairo last week that they should enter the war before the end of the year. In regard to Rhodes and the Dodecanese, although not operationally essential, it would clearly be desirable to clean up the islands as soon as possible and the idea should appeal to the Turks: (a) The Turks should be asked to say whether they are prepared to undertake the early capture of these islands; and (b) If they say they are unable to do this we should starve out the islands and occupy them later at our leisure."

12 November 1943. German Battle Group, including Brandenburger Parachute Regiment and commandos, assault Leros.

14-15 November 1943. Second Battalion Royal West Kent Regiment arrive from Samos to reinforce Leros garrison.

16 November 1943. Leros falls after what Churchill described as "Unexpectedly prolonged resistance." Brigadier Tilney surrenders at 2000 hrs.

18 November 1943. Churchill to Wilson: "Thank you for your messages about Leros. I approve your conduct of the operation."

Appendix III
Command Structure

BRITISH CHIEFS OF STAFF

Chief of the Imperial General Staff (Chairman of the Chiefs of Staff's Committee)	General Sir Alan Brooke (Field Marshal from Jan 1944)
Chief of the Air Staff	Air Chief Marshal Sir Charles Portal (Marshal of the Royal Air Force from Jan 1944)
First Sea Lord and Chief of the Naval Fleet	Admiral of the Fleet Dudley Pound (until Sept 1943), Admiral of the Fleet Sir Andrew Cunningham (from Oct 1943)
Deputy Secretary (Military) of the War Cabinet and Chief of Staff to the Minister of Defense	Lt-Gen Sir Hastings Ismay (General from May 1944)
Chief of Combined Operations	Maj-Gen RE Laycock (from Oct 1943)
Secretary	Maj-Gen LC Hollis

BRITISH VICE-CHIEFS OF STAFF

Vice-Chief of the Imperial General Staff	Lt-Gen AE (later Sir Archibald) Nye

| Vice-Chief of the Air Staff | Air Vice-Marshal Sir Douglas Evill (Air Marshal, 1944) |
| Vice-Chief of the Naval Staff | Vice-Admiral Sir Neville Syfret |

BRITISH JOINT STAFF MISSION IN WASHINGTON

| Head of the British Joint Staff Mission | Field Marshal Sir John Dill |

ALLIED EXPEDITIONARY FORCE, NORTHWEST EUROPE

Supreme Allied Commander	General Dwight D. Eisenhower (US)
Deputy Supreme Allied Commander	Air Chief Marshal Sir Arthur Tedder (Br)
Commander-in-Chief, Allied Naval Expeditionary Force	Admiral Sir Bertram Ramsay (Br)

ALLIED EXPEDITIONARY FORCES IN THE MEDITERRANEAN

Commander-in-Chief, Allied Expeditionary Forces	General Dwight D. Eisenhower (US)
Commander-in-Chief, Allied Naval Expeditionary Forces	Admiral of the Fleet Sir Andrew Cunningham (Br), Admiral Sir John Cunningham (Br) (from Sept 1943)
Commander-in-Chief, Fifteenth Army Group	General Sir Harold Alexander (Br)
Commander-in-Chief, Allied Air Forces	Air Chief Marshal Sir Arthur Tedder (Br)

MEDITERRANEAN COMMAND

| Supreme Allied Commander | General Sir Henry Maitland Wilson (Br) |
| Deputy Supreme Allied Commander | Lt-Gen JL Devers (US), Lt-Gen JT McNarney (US) (from Sept 1944) |

Commander-in-Chief, Allied Naval Forces	Admiral Sir John Cunningham (Br)
Commander-in-Chief, Mediterranean Allied Air Forces	Lt-Gen Ira C. Eaker (US) (Gen from Dec 1943)

MIDDLE EAST COMMAND

Commander-in-Chief (Army)	General Sir Henry Maitland Wilson (Br) (until Dec 1943)
Commander-in-Chief (Navy)	Admiral Sir Henry Harwood (Br)
Commander-in-Chief (Air)	Air Chief Marshal Sir Arthur Tedder (Br) (until Dec 1943)

Appendix IV
Allied Ships Taking Part
in Aegean Operations, 1943

Cruisers

HMS	Aurora	(1) Commodore EG Agnew, CB CVO DSO RN.
		(2) Capt G. Barnard, CBE DSO RN.
	Carlisle	Capt HF Nalder, RN.
	Dido	Capt J. Terry, MVO RN.
	Penelope	Capt CD Belben, DSC RN
	Phoebe	Capt CP Frend, RN.
	Sirius	Capt PWB Booking, DSO RN.

Fleet Destroyers

HMS	Echo	L/Cdr RHC Cyld, DSC RN.
	Eclipse	Cdr E. Mack, DSO DSC RN.
	Faulknor	(1) Capt AK Scott Moncrieff, DSO RN.
		(2) Capt MS Thomas, DSO RN.
	Fury	L/Cdr TF Taylor, DSC RN.
	Intrepid	Cdr CA de W. Kitcat, RN.
	Jervis	Capt JS Crawford, DSO RN.
	Panther	L/Cdr Viscount Jocelyn, RN.
	Pathfinder	L/Cdr CW Malins, DSO DSC RN.
	Petard	Cdr RC Egan, DSO DSC RN.
	Tumult	L/Cdr N. Lanyon, DSO DSC RN.
HHMS	Queen Olga	L/Cdr G. Glessas, DSO RHN.

Hunt Destroyers

HMS	Aldenham	L/Cdr JI Jones, DSO DSC RNR.
	Beaufort	Lt JRL Moore, RN.
	Belvoir	Lt JFD Bush, DSC RN.
	Blencathra	Lt EG Warren, RN.

Hunt Destroyers (Continued)

	Croome	L/Cdr HDM Slater, RN.
	Dulverton	Cdr SA Buss, MVO RN.
	Exmoor	Cdr J. Jeffreys, DSC RN.
	Hambledon	L/Cdr GW McKendrick, RN.
	Haydon	L/Cdr RC Watkins, RN.
	Hursley	L/Cdr WJP Church, DSO DSC RN.
	Hurworth	Cdr RH Wright, DSC RN.
	Lamerton	L/Cdr GTS Gray, DSC RN.
	Penn	L/Cdr JH Swain, DSO DSC RN.
	Rockwood	Lt SR Le H. Lombard-Hobson, RN.
	Tetcott	L/Cdr AF Harkness, OBE DSC RNR.
	Wilton	Lt GG Marten, RN.
HHMS	Adrias	Cdr JN Toumbas, RHN.
	Kanaris	Cdr Zartas, RHN.
	Miaoulis	(1) Cdr C Nikitiases, RHN.
		(2) Cdr E. Boudouris, RHN.
	Pindos	L/Cdr D. Fifas, RHN.
	Themistocles	L/Cdr N. Sarris, RHN.
ORP	Krakowiak	Cdr Naracewisz.

Submarines

HMS	Rorqual	L/Cdr LW Napier, DSO DSC RN.
	Seraph	Lt NLA Jewell, MBE DSC RN.
	Severn	L/Cdr ANG Campbell, RN.
	Shakespeare	Lt MFR Ainslie, DSO DSC RN.
	Sibyl	Lt EJD Turner, DSO DSC RN.
	Sickle	Lt JR Drummond, DSO DSC RN.
	Simoon	Lt GDN Milner, RN.
	Sportsman	Lt R. Gatehouse, DSC RN.
	Surf	Lt D. Lambert, DSC RN.
	Torbay	Lt RJ Clutterbuck, DSC RN.
	Trespasser	Lt RM Favell, DSC RN.
	Trooper	Lt JS Wraith, RN.
	Unrivalled	Lt HB Turner, DSC RN.
	Unruly	Lt JP Fyfe, DSC RN.
	Unsparing	Lt AD Piper, RN.
HHMS	Katsonis	Cdr Lascos, RHN.
ORP	Dzik	Cdr Romanowski.
	Sokol	L/Cdr GC Koziolkowski.

Coastal Craft and Raiding Forces	-	15
Motor Torpedo Boats - 10th Flotilla	-	7
Motor Gunboats - Part of 60th Flotilla	-	3
Minesweepers	-	4
Motor Launches - 24th and 42nd Flotillas	-	16
Total Ships, Submarines and Other Craft:		97

Losses: 32 vessels, or 33 percent of the total.

Source: <u>ADM 234/364</u>.

Appendix V
Comprehensive List of Allied Ships Lost, Damaged, and Captured in Aegean Operations, 1943

Date	Ship	Status	Cause	Location
14 Sept	Katsonis, Greek submarine	Sunk	A/S	Aegean
26 Sept	Intrepid, destroyer	Sunk	A/C	Leros
26 Sept	Queen Olga, Greek destroyer	Sunk	A/C	Leros
3 Oct	LCT 3	Lost	---	Kos
7 Oct	Penelope, cruiser	Damaged	A/C	Scarpanto
9 Oct	Carlisle, cruiser	Damaged beyond repair	A/C	Scarpanto Strait
9 Oct	Panther, destroyer	Sunk	A/C	Scarpanto
11 Oct	ML 835	Sunk	A/C	---
12 Oct	Unrivalled, submarine	Damaged	D/C	
16 Oct	Torbay, submarine	Damaged	D/C	
17 Oct	Trooper, submarine	Lost	Mine	Leros
17 Oct	Sirius, cruiser	Damaged	A/C	Scarpanto
17 Oct	Hursley, destroyer	Damaged	Gunfire	Kalymnos
17 Oct	Hedgehog, schooner	Captured	Engine trouble	Levita
17 Oct	MTB 113	Damaged	---	---
19 Oct	Hurworth, destroyer	Sunk	Mine	Kalymnos
21 Oct	ML 1015	Lost	Foundered	
22 Oct	Adrias, destroyer (Greek)	Damaged	Mine	Kalymnos
24 Oct	Eclipse, destroyer	Sunk	Mine	Karabakla Channel
26 Oct	ML 579	Sunk	A/C	Lipso
28 Oct	LCT 115	Sunk	A/C	Kastellorizo
30 Oct	Aurora, cruiser	Damaged	A/C	Kastellorizo
31 Oct	Unsparing, submarine	Damaged	Gunfire	
11 Nov	Rockwood, destroyer	Damaged	A/C	---
11 Nov	LCM 923	Captured	---	Leros

11--12 Nov	BYMS 72	Captured	---	Kalymnos
12 Nov	ML 358	Sunk	Gunfire	Leros
12 Nov	ML 456	Damaged	Gunfire	---
13 Nov	Dulverton, destroyer	Sunk	A/C	Gulf of Kos
15 Nov	Simoon, submarine	Sunk	Mine	Dardandelles
16 Nov	Unseen, submarine	Damaged	D/C	
16 Nov	Penn, destroyer	Damaged	Gunfire	

Source: ADM Casualty Lists.

Glossary:

A/S	Anti-submarine Craft.
A/C	Aircraft.
D/C	Depth Charges.

Selected Bibliography

United States Government Archives.

Archives of the Department of the Army, Office of the Chief of Military History, General Reference Branch, Historical Services Division, Washington, DC: The Casualties of the US Armed Forces, World War II and GA Harrison, Cross Channel Attack, 1951.

United Kingdom. British Government Archives.

Public Record Office (PRO).
Admiralty (ADM Series).
Air Ministry (AIR Series).
Cabinet and Cabinet Committees (CAB Series).
War Office (WO Series).
War Premier's Personal Papers (PREM Series).

United Kingdom: British Information Srevices.

The Strength and Casualties of the Armed Forces and Auxiliary Services of the United Kingdom, 1939-1945; Monograph, ID672. Based on White Paper of 6 June 1946. New York: Rockefeller Plaza, June 1946.

Published Government Records and Official Histories.

Buckley, Christopher. Five Ventures. United Kingdom Military Series. Popular Military History Series by various authors. London: Her Majesty's Stationery Office, 1954.

Ehrman, John. Grand Strategy, Vol. 5, August 1943-September 1944. United Kingdom Military Series. JRM Butler, gen. ed., History of the Second World War. London: Her Majesty's Stationery Office, 1956.

Molony, CJC, et al. The Mediterranean and Middle East, vol. 5. United Kingdom Military Series. JRM Butler, gen. ed., History of the Second World War. London: Her Majesty's Stationery Office, 1973.

Rowan-Robinson, H. The Surrender of Italy. Monograph. Short History of the Second World War. Royal United Services Institute. London: His Majesty's Stationery Office, 1943.

Personal Interviews and Correspondence.

Lt-Col R Butler; Jack Dimitriadis; David Eisenhower; Mrs Diana French; L Marsland Gander; Captain J. James; Rt Hon The Earl Jellicoe; Rt Hon Tom King MP; Lt-Col RF Kirby; Major-General DL Lloyd Owen; Captain JR Newmark; Brigadier JJJ Phipps; Brigadier GL Prendergast; Air Marshal HA Probert; Brigadier JS Ryder; Major-General JM Strawson; Colonel David Sutherland; Professor AJP Taylor; Brigadier RA Tilney; Colonel TIM Waugh; The Hon CM Woodhouse; and The Rev Canon GM Young.

Memoirs, Speeches, Papers, and Biographies.

Bryant, Sir Arthur. The Turn of the Tide: A History of the War Years based on the Diaries of Field-Marshal Lord Alanbrooke, Chief of the Imperial General Staff. New York: Doubleday, 1957.

---.Triumph in the West. A History of the War Years based on the Diaries of Field-Marshal Lord Alanbrooke, Chief of the Imperial General Staff. New York: Doubleday, 1959.

Churchill, Winston S. The Hinge of Fate. The Second World War. 6 Vols. Boston: Houghton, Mifflin, 1950.

---.Closing the Ring. The Second World War. 6 Vols. Boston: Houghton, Mifflin, 1951.

Howard, Michael. The Mediterranean Strategy in the Second World War. The Lee-Knowles Lectures delivered by Michael Howard at the University of Cambridge, England, 1966. New York: Frederick A. Praeger, Inc., 1968.

Ismay, Lord. The Memoirs of General Lord Ismay. London: William Heinemann, 1960.

Pogue, Forrest C. George C. Marshall: Organizer of Victory, 1943-1945. New York: The Viking Press, 1973.

Wilson, Henry Maitland, Bt. Eight Years Overseas, 1939-1947. London: Hutchinson, 1948.

General and Specialized Studies.

Barker, Elisabeth. Churchill and Eden at War. London: Mac Millan, 1978.

Brown, Anthony Cave. Bodyguard of Lies. New York: Bantam Books, 1976, published by arrangement with Harper & Row, London, 1975.

Colville, John. The Fringes of Power. London: Hodder & Stoughton, 1985.

Gander, Marsland L. The Long Road to Leros. London: MacDonald, 1945.

Hastings, Max. Bomber Command. London: Michael Joseph, 1979.

Hastings, Max. Overlord. London: Michael Joseph, 1984.

---.The Korean War. New York: Simon & Schuster, 1987.

Heller, Mikhail, and Nekrich, Aleksander. Utopia in Power. New York: Summit Books, a Division of Simon & Schuster, 1986.

Hinsley, FH. British Intelligence in the Second World War, vol. 3, Pt. 1. Cambridge: Cambridge University Press, 1979.

Irving, David. Hitler's War. New York: The Viking Press, 1985.

Lloyd Owen, DL. Providence Their Guide. London: George Harrap, 1980.

Pitt, Barrie. Special Boat Squadron. London: Century Publishing, 1983.

Smith, Peter, and Walker, Edwin. War in the Aegean. London: William Kimber, 1974.

Spaeter, Helmet. Die Brandenburger. Munich: Walther Angerer, 1978.

Stoler, Mark A. The Politics of the Second Front: American Military Planning and Diplomacy in Coalition Warfare, 1941-1943, (Contributions in Military History, No. 12). Westport, Conn.: Greenwood Press, 1977.

Taylor, AJP. English History 1914-1945. Oxford: Oxford University Press, 1965.

Articles.

Drinkwater, William. "Leros Finale." The Military Chest, Vol.
4, No. 3. Corsham, Wiltshire: Picton Press, May/June 1985.

Lucas, James. "Strike on Leros." The Elite, No. 36. London:
Orbis Publishing, 1985.

Terraine, John.   "Who Bore the Brunt?"   World War II
Investigator, vol 1., no. 1. Hounslow Middlesex: World War II
Investigator, Ltd., 1988.

Index

Recent Titles in
Contributions in Military Studies
Series Advisor: Colin Gray

The American War in Vietnam: Lessons, Legacies, and Implications for Future Conflicts
Lawrence E. Grinter and Peter M. Dunn, editors

Nuclear War and Nuclear Strategy: Unfinished Business
Stephen J. Cimbala

The Anglo-American Winter War with Russia, 1918-1919: A Diplomatic and
Military Tragicomedy
Benjamin D. Rhodes

The Last Gaiter Button: A Study of the Mobilization and Concentration of the
French Army in the War of 1870
Thomas J. Adriance

NATO Strategy and Nuclear Defense
Carl H. Amme

A Nuclear-Weapon-Free Zone in the Middle East: Problems and Prospects
Mahmoud Karem

Gentlemen of the Blade: A Social and Literary History of the British Army Since 1660
G. W. Stephen Brodsky

China's Military Modernization: International Implications
Larry M. Wortzel

The Painful Field: The Psychiatric Dimension of Modern War
Richard A. Gabriel

The Spit-Shine Syndrome: Organizational Irrationality in the American Field Army
Christopher Bassford

Behind a Curtain of Silence: Japanese in Soviet Custody, 1945-1956
William F. Nimmo

Armed Forces on a Northern Frontier: The Military in Alaska's History, 1867-1987
Jonathan M. Nielson